CW01187874

LEGIONS IN CRISIS

LEGIONS IN CRISIS

TRANSFORMATION OF THE ROMAN SOLDIER AD 192–284

PAUL ELLIOTT

FONTHILL

Learn more about Fonthill Media. Join our mailing list to
find out about our latest titles and special offers at:
www.fonthillmedia.com

Fonthill Media Limited
Fonthill Media LLC
www.fonthillmedia.com
office@fonthillmedia.com

First published in the United Kingdom and the United States of America 2014

British Library Cataloguing in Publication Data:
A catalogue record for this book is available from the British Library

Copyright © Paul Elliott 2014

ISBN 978-1-78155-334-3

The right of Paul Elliott to be identified as the author of this work has been asserted by him in accordance with the Copyright, Designs and Patents Act 1988.

All rights reserved. No part of this publication may be reproduced, stored in a retrieval system or transmitted in any form or by any means, electronic, mechanical, photocopying, recording or otherwise, without prior permission in writing from Fonthill Media Limited

Typeset in 10pt on 13pt Sabon LT Std
Printed and bound in England

Contents

Acknowledgements

I would like to thank a number of people who have offered photographs, advice or commentary on the book or who helped develop some of the ideas within it. These include Dr Robert Mason from the Royal Ontario Museum (which houses some of the Dura Europus collection), Alexandra Croom of the Tyne & Wear Archives & Museums, Dr Mike Bishop with whom I discussed the survival of *lorica segmentata* into the third century, Robert Vermaat who as always has been a ready source of good references and obscure papers, Dr Ross Cowan, Graham Sumner, Nathan Ross as well as Jamie McLean (with whom I toured Rome in 2012). Ten years ago Paul Carrick introduced me to 'Quinta', the third century re-enactment group based at Arbeia Roman Fort and Museum and I have never forgotten his help and generosity. Florian Himmler has likewise provided inspiration and advice in the field of third century reconstruction; several of the colour plates were generously provided by him. Megan Doyon of Yale University's Ancient Art Department skilfully organised copyright issues on my behalf surrounding photographs from the Dura collection. For location photography in North Wales I thank Graham Sumner.

My wife Christine deserves a mention. For twenty years she has accompanied me to hundreds of Roman sites throughout Britain, Egypt, Greece and Italy ... thank you!

Introduction

'...things seemed hopeless and almost the whole Roman Empire had been lost,'
Eutropius, Breviarium 9.9

The third century AD was a turbulent and testing time for the Roman Empire. A new and powerful foe in the east had risen up to challenge Rome directly. Barbarians on the northern frontiers were now more aggressive and more numerous than before and internally the population of the empire had to contend with rampant inflation and a series of terrible plagues. Pressure on Rome was now relentless and constant. Perhaps a single, capable ruler could have steered the empire on a safe course through these storms. Unfortunately, the chaos became magnified by a lack of continuity on the imperial throne. The army had become powerful enough that either it chose some pliant aristocrat to be emperor, or else one of its own tough soldiers (often of common origins) took control directly. Either way these emperors had no effective legitimacy and none could stay the course. From the assassination of Commodus (AD 192) to the accession of Diocletian (AD 284) the imperial throne saw thirty six occupants. Only four of those died from natural causes, the rest were either killed in battle, by the assassin's hand or by suicide.

The army had real political power in the third century, making and unmaking emperors as it saw fit. It had been aided in this by Septimius Severus, the African emperor who had won out in the civil wars following Commodus' assassination. He increased the army's pay and granted other privileges, he enlarged the Praetorian Guard, increased the number of legions and opened up command posts to men who were not of senatorial birth. Crucially Severus had promised a payment of gold to his troops if they supported his claim to the throne. This 'donative' was so substantial that henceforth, troops knew full well that any rival for the throne who came from their ranks would reward loyalty with coin. And he knew how to cultivate loyalty. On his death-bed in AD 211, Severus gave his sons the advice they would need to stay in power: 'give money to the soldiers, and scorn all other men.'

While the army gained rapidly in size, stature and political savvy during the reign of Septimius Severus, it also accelerated a material transformation.

Armour, shields, helmets, swords and javelins all began to be replaced with new styles. A change in clothing altered the appearance of the typical legionary even further. By the end of the third century and the start of the authoritarian reign of Diocletian, the legionary had lost his familiar curved rectangular shield, no longer relied on the *lorica segmentata* or wielded the *gladius* (the short Roman stabbing sword). Neither did he wear a helmet that looked recognisably 'Roman'. Yet these new-look Roman soldiers continued to dominate the battlefields of the empire for another two centuries.

Although emperor Severus did not kick-start this transformation, he presided over the empire just as the legions began to adopt both the new equipment and the new way of fighting. With his decision to enlarge and re-organise the legions Severus may have helped to spread the influence of this third century transformation.

Legions in Crisis looks closely at the new styles of arms and armour, comparing their construction, use and effectiveness to the more familiar types of Roman kit used by soldiers fighting the earlier Dacian and Marcomannic Wars. What did this transformation in military technology mean for the tactical choices used on the battlefield? A succession of emperors altered the organisation of the army piecemeal, reacting to immediate military threats to provide a flexibility that met the tremendous challenges of the age. We analyse the changes that Severus himself made and look at their impact on the Roman army as a whole. Did the higher levels of pay, the new conditions and the re-organisation also indicate a change of strategy?

The third century crisis certainly cried out for a new way of waging way. It seems that, in forts and on battlefields across the Roman Empire, the soldiers of Severus and their descendants were able to find the tools they needed to wage this war. Although the outcome had looked in doubt, the army and the empire it protected weathered the storm to emerge into the fourth century fully able to tackle the challenges of a new age.

Map of the Northern Provinces.

Map of the Eastern Provinces and the Frontier with Persia.

List of Emperors

This list covers the reigning emperors of the second and third centuries. Co-emperors who do not outlast their partner appear in parentheses.

Date (AD)	Emperor
98–117	Trajan
117–138	Hadrian
138–161	Antoninus Pius
161–180	Marcus Aurelius
161–169	(Lucius Verus)
180–192	Commodus
193	Pertinax
193	Didius Julianus
193–211	Septimius Severus
211–217	Caracalla
211	(Geta)
217–218	Macrinus
218–222	Elagabalus
222–235	Alexander Severus
235–238	Maximinus Thrax
238	Gordian I
238	Gordian II
238	Pupienus and Balbinus
238–244	Gordian III
244–249	Philip 'the Arab'
249–251	Decius
251–253	Trebonianus Gallus
253	Aemilius Aemilianus
253–260	Valerian
260–268	Gallienus
268–270	Claudius II 'Gothicus'

270	Quintillus
270–275	Aurelian
275–276	Tacitus
276	Florianus
276–282	Probus
282–283	Carus
283–284	(Numerian)
283–285	Carinus
284–305	Diocletian

Rulers of the Gallic Empire

Date (AD)	Emperor
260–269	Postumus
269	Laelianus
269	Marius
269–271	Victorinus
271–274	Tetricus

1

Rise of Septimius Severus

'"You have trained under actual combat conditions in your continuous skirmishes with the barbarians, and you are accustomed to endure all kinds of labour. Ignoring heat and cold, you cross frozen rivers on the ice; you do not drink water from wells, but water you have dug yourself. You have also trained by fighting with animals, and, all in all, you have won so distinguished a reputation for bravery that no one could stand against you. Toil is the true test of the soldier, not easy living, and those luxury-loving sots would not face your battle cry, much less your battle line..." After Severus had finished speaking, the soldiers shouted his praises, calling him Augustus ... and displaying the utmost zeal and enthusiasm for him.'

Herodian II.10

While chill February winds whipped around the towers and wall-walks of the legionary fortress, an old man lay dying in the luxuriously furnished house that belonged to its commander. He was in his sixties, yet he was still strong-minded, ebullient and able to talk with both his advisors and his two attentive sons. The old man was Septimius Severus, emperor of Rome. He was far from that city, living with his vast staff of advisors and courtiers, at the centre of the fortress in Eboracum, northern Britannia.[1] Here 5,000 soldiers lived and worked, and were currently resting after fierce fighting in far flung Caledonia. But Severus liked to be surrounded by soldiers, even on his death-bed he would have found the idea comforting. It was the common men of the legions that had elevated him to the throne, followed him into battle and criss-crossed the empire to fight for his glory and his favour.

Even though these soldiers would die to preserve their emperor's life, there were doubts about others who stood in his bed-chamber. Dio Cassius, a senator and advisor on the campaign, remembered hearing rumours that Antoninus, the emperor's eldest son, had tried to hasten his father's death. Another historian, Herodian, stated bluntly that the treacherous Antoninus had actually bribed the court physicians to bring this about.[2]

With death clutching at him, Septimius Severus had a final meeting with his squabbling sons. Both had been proclaimed as heirs and joint co-emperors, but both were intensely fearful that when the time came the other would seize the throne for himself. Dio relates to us 'without embellishment' the emperor's last words of advice to his sons. The secret of his success in war, justice, politics and administration was summarized simply with the advice: 'agree with each other, give money to the soldiers, and scorn all other men.'

There was little chance of his sons getting on, as events later that year would show, but his last two recommendations were ruthlessly implemented by Antoninus and by successive emperors throughout the third century. Simply put, Severus was telling his sons to lavish money and attention on the legions in order to secure their loyalty. He had done this himself in order to fight off rivals in a civil war. Severus could not call on dynastic loyalties, he could only call on the military barrack-room loyalties of soldiers who had served under him as governor. But those loyalties were always fickle, and maintained by gold and battlefield plunder. To retain the throne he had learnt to cultivate his relationship with the legions in a way that no emperor had done before. He dearly hoped that his successors would do as well in the dark days that were to come.

On 4 February 211, Lucius Septimius Severus, the twenty-first emperor of Rome died. The dynasty he established would last another twenty years before chaos and turmoil would reign...

Legions on the Danube

The source of emperor Severus' power came from the legions, but more specifically it came from the legions stationed on the Danube frontier. This set of provinces (Raetia, Noricum, Pannonia and Moesia) bound both the eastern and western halves of the empire together. They formed, along with their legions, a vital bulwark against which the belligerent tribes of Dacia and Germany crashed. Its legions were motivated and battle-hardened, and crucially for the fate of any would-be emperor, there were a lot of them.

Forty years of warfare on this Roman border had resulted in a massive build-up of military might. Further west the river Rhine acted as another frontier barrier and legions were also encamped there, ready to repulse frequent raids by German tribes. As pressure from northern tribes like the Quadi, Marcomanni, Naristi and Iazyges intensified, so did the Roman build-up. The Danubian army soon became the largest in the empire. During the on-going civil wars that would erupt throughout the third century the candidates that competed so violently for the throne more often than not were promoted by the soldiers garrisoned on the Danube. Maximinus I, for example, was an ex-legionary, risen through the ranks of a Danubian unit and he gained the support of his fellow-soldiers. From humble origins he become emperor of Rome. It was obvious that these legions held real power; at this crucial cross-roads in ancient history the fate of the empire rested on their shoulders.

It had not always been so. Emperors prior to 162 had only to deal with the German threat across the Rhine, and did so with a military force equal to the task. The river Danube flowing east formed a natural frontier that had been lightly protected, considering its length, and this had been up till now adequate protection. Indeed a new province, Dacia, had been carved out of barbarian territory across the Danube by emperor Trajan. In 162, however, and for a number of years afterwards, Germanic tribes invaded Roman territories, including the Danubian province of Raetia. Marcus Aurelius had two new legions recruited around 165 as an emergency measure, these would become Legio II Italica and Legio III Italica, garrisoned in Noricum and Raetia respectively.

The attacks worsened. In 166 and 167 tribes called the Langobardi, Ubii and Lacringi invaded Pannonia, whilst the Vandals and Iazyges attacked Dacia, killing the governor there. Marcus took his new legions northwards in 168 and so began a protracted campaign against the new barbarian threat. During these wars the barbarian armies crossed the Danube and ravaged parts of the empire, the Costoboci reaching as far south as Eleusis in Greece. Balomar, king of the fierce and well-organised Marcomanni even defeated 20,000 legionaries at Carnuntum in 170 before marching south into Italy to besiege the city of Aquileia. The Roman counter-offensive included both diplomacy and force, and by 180 most of the warring tribes had either been won over or subjugated.

In 180 Marcus Aurelius died while on campaign against the Quadi. His son Commodus had no interest in fighting the war and he left his generals, including Pescennius Niger and Clodius Albinus, to continue it in his absence.

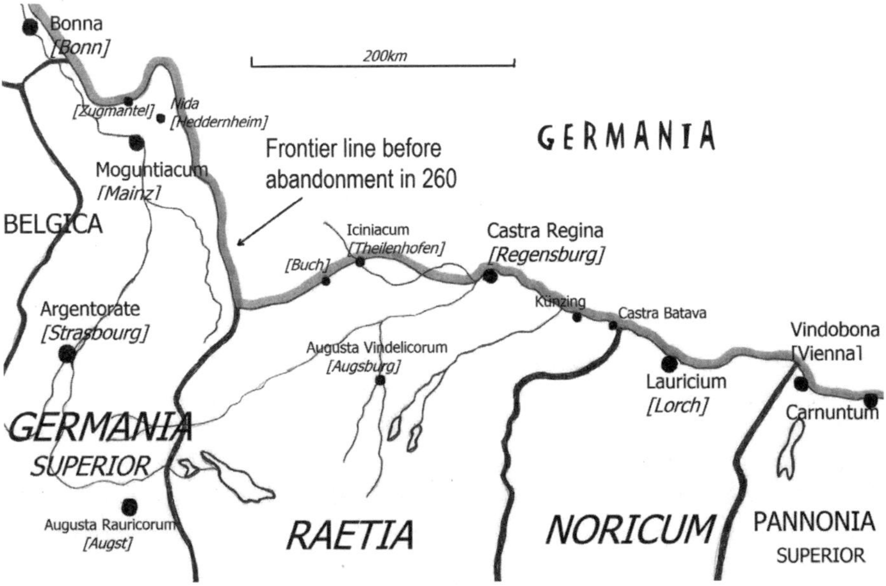

A decade of intense warfare on the doorstep of Italy had shown how vulnerable the empire was to a concerted attack. Yet these Marcomannic Wars were to be but a foretaste of the future barbarian migrations that would end with the collapse of the western half of the empire three centuries later. The threat to Rome was soberly understood, however, resulting, by the end of the Marcomannic Wars, in half of the empire's military force being stationed behind the Rhine and the Danube. This constituted sixteen out of the empire-wide total of thirty legions.

It was in the year of Marcus Aurelius' death that a thirty-five-year-old senator from North Africa, Lucius Septimius Severus, gained his first military command. Septimius Severus took up the office of legate, the commanding officer in charge of Legio IV Scythica. Severus would later fight off opponents to become emperor himself, but while in Syria he made contacts, gained valuable experience and may have met his future wife, Julia Domna.

The IV Scythica was one of three legions in Syria, which was the crucial eastern province which held at bay the might of the belligerent Parthian Empire. Governing this wealthy, eastern province was Helvius Pertinax who will have worked closely with his three legionary commanders, including of course Septimius Severus. Legionaries of the IV Scythica will have visited forts and garrison towns along the eastern frontier, including the city of Dura Europus. It is likely that Severus, too, inspected these garrisons, to check on their preparedness should the Parthians choose to over-run the frontier during his time in office.[3]

As commander of the most prestigious of the Syrian legions, Severus may even have been acting governor for a short time. Pertinax, Severus and hundreds of men like them across the empire were of the senatorial class and not soldiers by birth. They competed for better and more prestigious public offices, both administrative and military, in their pursuit of status, wealth and respect. Pertinax, when he was around Severus' age, had secured for himself command of the Roman fleet on the Rhine, followed soon after by promotion to chief financial officer (procurator) of the Dacian province. The much younger Septimius Severus was similarly eager to climb the 'ladder of honours' in search of fame and fortune.

Both Pertinax and Severus later received the governorship of provinces in the western half of the empire, the former of Britannia, the latter of Lugdunensis (southern France). During Septimius' tenure as governor his wife died and, in 187, he made contact with the high priest of Emesa in Syria to ask for the hand of one of his two daughters in marriage. This was Julia Domna, who sailed to Lugdunensis in order to marry Septimius Severus in the summer. By 192 Pertinax had risen to the position of Prefect of the City and then to consul of Rome in partnership with the young emperor Commodus. Severus, meanwhile, had been made governor of Upper Pannonia. Such an appointment was unexpected. This province, which lay along the vulnerable Danubian frontier, was home to three tough battle-tested legions and no large troop concentration lay nearer to Italy.[4] The command of such a crucial concentration of legions had rarely been given to men who had not earned that position first through the successful governance of several other key provinces. Almost simultaneously Severus' brother, Septimius Geta, was appointed governor of Lower Moesia, another key Danubian province with two legions of its own. Responsible for the appointment of Septimius Severus was the new commander of the Praetorian Guard, Aemilius Laetus. Perhaps it was no surprise that he hailed from North Africa too, one of a growing number of North African Romans of influence and power within Commodus' government.

North Africa was not some backwater of empire at this point, it was a thriving region that provided a large proportion of Rome's grain. Over three centuries earlier the powerful city of Carthage had dominated North Africa and fought three wars with Rome for control of the western Mediterranean. Carthage had been defeated and not just defeated but dismantled and destroyed, its cropland salted and cursed. Over the past three centuries however, newly established Roman provinces in North Africa grew and steadily developed. By the time of Marcus Aurelius, educated and wealthy Roman Africans were reaching great heights, whether they were descended from Italian settlers or old Carthaginian notables.

It may be that Laetus was indeed motivated by native loyalty, or perhaps he simply chose the best man for the job. Whatever his motivations, his choice had extraordinary repercussions on the fate of the empire and on the legions that protected it.

Severus Takes Rome

Commodus, son and heir of Marcus Aurelius who had fought so hard to prevent the northern frontiers from being overrun in the Marcomannic Wars, was a vain, cruel, paranoid fantasist about which none of the ancient writers had anything good to say. There had been several failed plots against his life, it was only a matter of time before one of them would succeed. The Prefect of the Guard, Laetus, and the emperor's chamberlain, Eclectus, were instrumental in the assassination of Commodus on New Year's Eve 192. When the poison he was tricked into consuming merely made him ill, the athlete Narcissus was sent in to finish the job by strangulation. One ancient source implicates another influential individual in the murder: Helvius Pertinax. As consul of Rome it was Pertinax who now stood forward to claim the imperial throne. He made a speech within the walls of the Praetorian camp which was the home of the imperial bodyguard. Offering each soldier 12,000 sesterces and announcing that Commodus had died suddenly of natural causes, he asked for the loyalty of the Praetorian Guard. There was hesitation and a little resistance but the troops eventually came around to Pertinax and acclaimed him emperor. Without their support he stood no chance since the Praetorians had gained a reputation in years gone by as masters of the throne. Several emperors owed their good fortunes (and lives) to the whim of these imperial bodyguards. Past emperors Domitian, Otho and Claudius all owed their places on the throne to the actions of the Guard, while the emperors Galba and Vitellius died at the hands of disgruntled Praetorians. When emperors passed on the empire to a nominated successor the Guard had been happy to transfer its loyalty to the new incumbent, whether a blood relative or an adopted heir. In times of dynastic uncertainty, however, the Praetorians were keen to impose their will, or at least receive some kind of payment for their loyalty.

The elevation of Pertinax to the imperial throne proved to be one of those times of 'dynastic uncertainty', and although the Guard had been bought off, the loyalty that it purchased would not last for long. The sixty-six year-old emperor tried to change too much, too quickly and crucially attempted to curb some of the excesses of the Praetorian Guard. Resentment against Pertinax grew quickly with the inevitable result that the Guard turned against him. On 28 March three hundred soldiers burst into the imperial palace on the Palatine Hill to challenge the emperor. Despite his attempts to appease them, the Praetorians killed him with their swords. His reign had lasted only eighty-seven days.

The uncertainty created by Commodus remained, there had to be an emperor, but whoever stepped forward had first to deal with the fickle Praetorians. The soldiers returned to the Praetorian Camp fearful of the public reaction, no obvious candidate existed for them to elevate to the purple ... and so heralds on the walls of the camp announced the public sale of the throne and not one, but two buyers came forward! Of the two, Flavius Sulpicianus (Pertinax's father-in-law) and Didius Julianus (a wealthy and respected senator), it was the latter who won the auction. However, the Praetorian's choice did not prove popular with either the people, the senate or, in the end, the Praetorians themselves. They soon tired of Julianus who did not appear to have the means to honour his lavish promises.

Other candidates for the throne had declared themselves upon hearing the news of the death of Pertinax. Yet these candidates had nothing to do with the sordid auction within the Praetorian Camp, or with attempts to flatter or bribe the imperial bodyguard. These three claimants to the throne were governors in provinces that were home to powerful military contingents and all had a good chance of seizing power. The governor of Syria, Pescennius Niger, was proclaimed emperor in mid-April by the four legions under his command. Later that month Clodius Albinus, the governor of Britannia, also claimed the throne. He had three legions to back up his claim. However, a candidate with some serious military backing had already emerged. Septimius Severus was governor of Upper Pannonia and proclaimed emperor by his troops on 9 April, barely two weeks after the murder of Pertinax. Not only did Severus enjoy the loyalty of the three legions under his provincial command, he had also managed to secure the support of all the legions on both Rhine and Danube frontiers. This amounted to a combined force of sixteen legions, should he dare to mobilize them all.

Having the strongest hand in the game and being the closest to Rome, Severus marched on the capital. Didius Julianus, with the nervous support of the senate, made attempts to defend the city from attack, but with little real success. As Severus and his legions approached the city the senate hastily passed a motion that sentenced Didius Julianus to death and it also bestowed divine honours on the dead emperor Pertinax. Its membership was well aware of the friendship between the murdered emperor and the approaching general. Julianus was summarily executed by an officer; he had ruled Rome for only sixty-six days.

Severus and his army entered Rome without opposition. He was now emperor of Rome and he took the name of Pertinax as part of his own imperial title. What did the Praetorian Guard do about this turn of events? By the time Severus crossed the city boundaries, the Guard had already been disbanded. He knew full well that although the imperial bodyguard might be overawed by the number of troops he had brought with him to secure his claim, months or years down the line they may have a Fate in store for him not too dissimilar to the onc they had meted out to Pertinax. Of course Septimius Severus had to be seen to punish the murderers of Pertinax and that was quickly achieved – the men involved were surrendered to him.

To deal with the Guard, he had to be clever and avoid an armed confrontation. Severus asked the Praetorians to pay homage to him in ceremonial dress (that is in off-duty attire, without swords, helmets or armour). When they paraded outside Rome in front of him, Severus then ordered his loyal troops to strip the Praetorians of their military belts, their daggers, uniforms and military insignia. All of the assembled Praetorians were formally discharged and instructed never to set foot in Rome again. The cavalrymen had to let their horses loose, although one horse followed its rider in a stubborn refusal to leave him. The Praetorian was forced to kill the horse and then himself. Thus the Guard was disbanded without a fight.

East and West

Writers sympathetic to Severus claim that the people of Rome celebrated his entrance into the city with garlands, burning torches and incense.[5] The more clear headed Historia Augusta records how the new emperor brought his legions with him, first he made sacrifices at the Capitol, then he moved on to the imperial palace. The thousands of troops had to be billeted across the city in temples, porticoes and shrines, and it appears that they behaved badly, taking what they wanted by force and threatening to lay the city waste.

Matters of state were rapidly dealt with and coins were issued. It must be remembered that for any new emperor coinage acted as a tool of propaganda, and allowed the newcomer to advertise his authority and legitimacy to the man on the street. There was little time to waste in Rome, however, Severus had two rivals for the throne itching to replace him. The first was governor of Britain, Clodius Albinus, whom Severus had already contacted and appeased with a share of the imperial throne. Technically now there were two emperors both issuing their own triumphant coinage, yet both knew the day would come when they would have to meet on some remote battlefield to fight for the throne.

Of more urgent importance was his other rival, Pescennius Niger, the governor of Syria who had been acclaimed emperor by his troops but who had remained in Antioch to gather support and build up his army. Less than thirty days after arriving in the capital, Severus and his armies were hurriedly marching east to intercept Niger's forces at the earliest opportunity.

Battles between the two forces occurred throughout western Anatolia at Perinthus, Cyzicus, Nicaea and at least one of the passes through the Taurus mountains. By fortifying these passes Niger hoped to protect the northern flank of Syria and his capital at Antioch. Beaten back, he was forced to retreat to that city where he found that support for his cause was beginning to fall away; some of the eastern cities and some of the Roman governors had begun to switch their allegiance. The governor of Arabia, for example, was a native of Perinthus which Niger had attempted to capture. The decisive battle occurred at Issus, where Alexander the Great had defeated a Persian army more than five hundred years earlier. The Severan forces were helped by a thunderstorm which drove rain into the faces of Niger's legions. Demoralised and retreating, they were ultimately caught in the rear by Severan cavalry which scattered the eastern legions and caught them on the run. The writer Dio claims that Niger's forces lost 20,000 men in the battle. Niger himself was cornered and beheaded. The rest of 194 was taken up with settling debts, punishing the supporters of Niger and putting his own men in command of the eastern provinces and their legions.

In the spring of 195 Severus launched an attack into northern Mesopotamia, across the Euphrates river in order to punish the Parthian kingdom for its support of Niger. Surviving forces of the defeated Pescennius Niger had fled eastwards and found sanctuary within Parthian territory. Parthia had to be punished; that was the official line. The writer Dio claims that the entire expedition was conceived 'out of a desire for glory'. Parthia was 'the East' and will dominate the narrative of this book. Emperors and generals like Crassus, Trajan and Mark Anthony campaigned in the east to secure glory and stature in the eyes of both Rome and of their own soldiers; Severus was no different. After a bloody civil war he may have wanted to give his troops (both western and defeated eastern) the opportunity to fight side by side, earn some victories and gain some plunder. It was during this period that two new legions, I Parthica and III Parthica, were brought up to strength, probably from the recruits hastily assembled by Niger in the east during his preparations. They would be trained and led by a core of veterans released from the Danubian legions.

During 195 his legions fought at least three major battles against Arab and Adiabeni forces. In response the senate began arrangements back in Rome to construct a triumphal arch for the emperor. While on campaign Severus took the bold step of naming Antoninus, his seven year-old son, 'Caesar' – that is, junior co-ruler and heir to the throne. This was a direct challenge to Clodius Albinus in Britain who was now cut out of the succession. Severus decided the time was right to move on his western rival and he began the march back to Rome.

During 196 Clodius Albinus crossed the Channel to Gaul with his own legions (around 40,000 men in total) and began his push to Italy. When he found the Alpine passes blocked he based himself at Lugdunum and began to raise additional forces there. On 19 February 197 the armies of Albinus and Severus met in battle on the outskirts of the city. It was no foregone conclusion, the size of the opposing armies was surprisingly well matched and Severus at one point was thrown off his horse; to avoid being identified and killed he tore off his purple cloak that would identify him as emperor. The arrival of Severan cavalry saved the situation and the battle swung against Albinus. Fleeing inside Lugdunum with some of his troops to escape the enemy, Albinus was forced to commit suicide. In an act of cruel pleasure Severus had his rival's head cut off and sent to Rome before laying out the naked body and riding his horse over it. As an end to the matter the bodies of Clodius Albinus, his wife and his sons were thrown into the river Rhône.

Septimius Severus was now emperor without rival, with an heir designate and an army that had known nothing but victory. For this restless commander the rest of 197 was taken up with organising his unified empire, rooting out the supporters of Albinus from a number of provinces and marching once more to the east. In a determined attack on the Parthian kingdom, the Roman forces were able to capture and sack its capital, Ctesiphon. The emperor spent five years organising his two new provinces (Osrhoene and Mesopotamia) and touring Judaea and Egypt. He returned to Rome in 202.

The Changes

The military changes that would mark Severus' reign and stand as a legacy throughout the third century began almost immediately. First – the Praetorian Guard. This force of around 8,000 soldiers provided a security force within Rome and provided a vital function, acting as bodyguard to the royal family and as a personal fighting unit on the battlefield. Traditionally open only to men of Italian birth, the Guard was quickly filled by Severus with deserving soldiers who had served in the northern legions. After this point Italians would no longer serve as Praetorians, more than half would come from western legions, the rest were recruited from units in the east. Most of those western legionaries would be Dalmatians and Pannonians. In a stroke Severus had removed a worrying threat and replaced it with a die-hard regiment of loyalist troops who loomed menacingly over Rome in his absence. The Guard still retained its power, however, and its elite membership were still keenly aware of this.[6]

Severus initiated other changes. Three new legions, Legio I, II and III Parthica were established. Recruitment for Legio II Parthica probably began immediately in 193. It was partly raised through conscription of Italian natives, a process called the *dilectus*, which attracted recruits with the prospect of good pay and the chance of promotion. This was unusual, few Italians marched with the legions anymore. New recruits were more commonly found within the province that a legion garrisoned, and, more often than not, these provinces were out on the frontier. With Legio II Severus smashed tradition and based the new regiment at Albanum barely 34 km from Rome. Up until this point no imperial legion had been allowed a base within Italy in order to prevent it threatening Rome. Troop numbers for Legio I and III Parthica seem to have been raised in the east sometime during the following year. Officers and centurions for these three new legions would need to have some experience and almost certainly came from the Danubian legions that had marched to Rome with their emperor. Not only did this provide a core of military experience at the heart of each new legion, but it also ensured a level of personal loyalty to the emperor from soldiers who had elevated him to that position.

Contemporary writers were greatly concerned by the close proximity of Legio II Parthica to the capital, it represented the abandonment of a long-standing tradition that Romans considered important. At a distance of 34 km (23 Roman miles) it could easily be argued that the legion was positioned to intervene in Rome's affairs at any time. Writing on military matters in the fourth century AD, Vegetius advises that Roman soldiers should be trained to march 24 Roman miles in five hours, 'at the full step', putting Legio II within five hours march of the capital. Was this an act of intimidation or one of defence? Opinion is divided.

Of more personal interest to the soldiers themselves, Severus gave his troops the right to marry. They had previously been able to have relationships with local women, unrecognized in law, and some maintained these partnerships through many years and several postings. Children were born within these relationships, but all were illegitimate. Marriage provided the wife with the legal right to her late husband's estate and it legitimised his offspring. Such a move would have been good for morale and bolstered the opinion of Severus amongst his troops.

The grant to marry while in service was not the only popular appeal to the soldiery. For the first time since emperor Domitian (AD 81–96) Severus raised the annual pay of the legionary from 300 to 450 denarii. Likewise the auxiliary soldier saw his pay climb from 100 to 150 denarii. Legionary cavalry pay rose from 400 to 600 denarii, auxiliary cavalry pay rose from around 200 to around

300 denarii if part of a cohort, or from 333 to 500 denarii if part of a cavalry wing. Severus' son Caracalla later followed suit after his father's death, increasing pay so that it was double the value it had been during Commodus' reign. Any increase was overdue; inflation had left the soldiers' pay standing and increased the chance of the troops rallying to any leader who promised a donative (a one-off gift of money) should they fight for him in any civil war. Yet these large increases in pay cost the imperial treasury dearly, resulting in a debasement of the coinage.

Although these reforms resembled gifts bestowed on the legions by a grateful emperor, they did not destabilise the relationship between army and state. Far more damage was done by the favour now shown to frontier troops. Recruited from frontier provinces to maintain the manpower of legions stationed there, new recruits were often effective fighters. However, they lacked the crucial understanding any Italian would have, that a soldier of Rome owes absolute loyalty to the remote SPQR, the 'Senate and the People of Rome' and of course, to the man at the head of it all, the emperor. Legions manned by frontier recruits had a different loyalty, to that general who would give them donatives or chances for war and plunder.

At the command level, loyalties were also being tested to breaking point. Many centurions serving within the legions had been promoted from the ranks of the Praetorian Guard in Rome. Most would be Italians, with a strong sense of allegiance to the emperor, to Rome and to its institutions. Now that provincials from Britain, the Rhine and Danube were dominating the barrack blocks of the Guard, promotion to the centurianate of a legion no longer carried with it that traditional allegiance.

Command of the legion was the responsibility of a senator. As a legionary legate, this would mark another rung on the senator's career ladder. Of course the senate embodied Rome, Roman values and Roman thinking – yet from the reign of Severus the number of senators receiving command positions began to drop until, by the reign of emperor Gallienus in 261, they were forbidden by statute to serve as legates at all. Instead the position was gradually opened up to the equestrians, a large ambitious class of wealthy families who were normally excluded from the privileges and responsibilities of government.

In all, Septimius Severus had aggrandised the legions, he was practising his own advice: 'give money to the soldiers, and scorn all other men.' Empowering the soldiers, in effect buying their loyalty with cash, promises and privileges, was crucial for the winner in a civil war, for if Severus could unseat an usurper so another chancer might just as easily march on Rome and do the same ... unless the rules were changed. Severus was changing the rules, closing the door to potential rivals. That was probably his intent at any rate but in doing this he was handing over the keys of the empire to the *miles*, the common soldier.[7]

Once Severus and his close kin were out of the picture the legions would not owe the new emperor any loyalties whatsoever. The seeds of disaster were sown.

2

New Strategies

'Posterity, which experienced the fatal effects of his maxims and example, justly considered [Septimius Severus] as the principle author of the decline of the Roman Empire.'

Edward Gibbon, *The Decline and Fall of the Roman Empire*

Historians have argued for decades that Septimius Severus not only contributed to the decline of the Roman Empire but that he may have been the architect of its downfall. Much of this discussion hinges on his military reforms. Seen over the course of succeeding centuries, his changes in military organisation may have been fundamental in shifting the Roman military might from a strategy of static frontier defence to one of central reserve forces.

It remains uncertain, however, whether Severus himself consciously planned to take the Roman army in this direction or whether he was in fact responding to immediate concerns of defence. The army that emerged one hundred years later would be based on a bipartite military organisation, this would differ significantly from the well-known array of legions that spread out along the empire's frontiers. The frontier of the fourth century Roman Empire would be settled by *limitanei* border garrisons, while more centrally located mobile field armies (*comitatenses*) would be ready to respond to threats from any direction.

Between Severus and this new strategic model, however, lay the battles and upheavals of the third century. Nothing was set in stone and nothing could be taken for granted. Historical hindsight induces a calm complacency, but for those living at the time, Rome ('the world') was being beaten back, overrun by adversity and faced imminent destruction. Individuals, not history or destiny, would carve out the empire's future... if it had one at all.

How the Legions Work

In 192 the defence of the Roman Empire was based around thirty legions, dispersed around the frontiers as needed. The legion was a corporate unit, with its own identity, traditions and battle honours. Its men were often fiercely proud of their legion, a relationship enjoyed today between a British soldier and his regiment.

In size each legion was similar, with a manpower of roughly 5,000 soldiers based around ten cohorts. These cohorts were commanded by senior centurions and were each formed up of six centuries. Despite the misleading title, the century was a combat unit of eighty men led by a highly paid centurion. Cohorts then, being six centuries in size, had a typical strength of 480 men. The cohort and the century were the real tactical units of any Roman force. A cohort may be ordered to 'follow the flag' to form a *vexillation* and join a larger unit needing extra manpower.

The eighty men of a century were billeted in 'tent parties' of eight men each, these soldiers would be squad-mates, eating and sleeping together, fighting together, sharing a tent on campaign and a set of twin rooms while in barracks. Centurions had their own staff, not only a servant or two, but also junior officers from the century such as the *tesserarius* (watch keeper), the *signifier* (standard bearer and unit treasurer) and the *optio* (the centurion's second-in-command). This unit proved quite self-sufficient, its men cooked their own meals and had entrenching tools, tents, arms and armour. It could draw mules from the legion to carry rations, equipment and other baggage and operate independently of its parent unit.

Some, and perhaps all, of the legions elevated the status and responsibility of the first cohort. The writer Vegetius reports that men of the first cohort were the tallest men in the legion.[1] Instead of six centuries the first cohort contained only five, although its centuries were kept at double strength (170 men under a single centurion, rather than eighty). This meant that the first cohort became a powerful unit of 800 soldiers, a formation that could be used to spearhead assaults. As the cohort of honour, 'the first' was no doubt filled with veterans from across the legion and its five centurions must have been the most senior within the regiment.

In command of a legion was a member of the senatorial order, a *legatus legionis*. He was a man in his thirties working his way from office to office and was aided by a young senatorial officer, a *tribunus laticlavius*, perhaps in his late teens or early twenties. He may hope to command a legion himself, later on in his career. Third in command was a seasoned centurion of long service, the *praefectus castrorum*, or camp prefect, responsible for logistics and administration. Like a senior NCO in any modern army, he will have been able to provide valuable tactical advice to the legionary legate. There were in addition, five young tribunes (*tribuni angusticlavii*) from Rome's equestrian class within the legion's headquarters. Without any specific command responsibility, they were given tasks as and when needed.

Each legion was allocated its own troop of 120 cavalry which carried out scouting, long range patrol, courier duties and screening the flanks of the legion if it was called on to march through hostile territory. Of course the cavalry also had its use in battle but typically this involved mopping up the enemy soldiers after the Roman legionaries had forced them to break and flee.

Additional forces were provided by auxiliary units (*auxilia*). Whereas legions were only open to Roman citizens (and popular with the poor and landless), the auxiliaries recruited non-citizens from recently conquered provinces. The bellicose tribes that had given the Romans so much trouble during the invasion and takeover of their homelands made ideal army material. Gauls, Germans, Britons, Dacians and others provided men for these auxiliary units.

The relationship between legion and *auxilia* could be compared to that of the International Security Assistance Forces (ISAF) and the Afghan National Army (ANA) in modern-day Afghanistan. Post-Taliban, the ANA was reformed and underwent training along NATO lines, using US uniforms and equipment. Patrols and assaults in Afghanistan have been conducted by both forces in concert, with ISAF troops taking the lead. Like the Roman *auxilia*, the ANA often provides support during assaults, but it is also able to conduct its own operations. The analogy cannot be stretched too far, but it gives an idea of the relationship and differing status between the two types of troops. A division of labour, trust and responsibility existed between legion and *auxilia*.[2]

Auxiliaries really were the junior partner in the military relationship. Pay for an auxiliary infantryman was 100 denarii compared to 300 for a legionary, for example. Auxiliary units were based around a single *quingenary* cohort (around 480 strong) or a double-sized *milliary* cohort (around 800 strong). This meant they could be moved easily around the empire as needed but it also pre-empted any troop rebellion. An aggrieved ethnic group now fighting for Rome as an auxiliary unit would have little chance against the higher level command structure and massed cohorts of a Roman legion. Auxiliary uprisings were very rare but did occur from time to time. ISAF troops, wary of individual ANA soldiers within their compounds, may sympathise with Roman legionaries who had no choice but to fight alongside men who had until recently been their sworn enemies ...[3]

Most Roman cavalry was provided by mounted *auxilia*, since many frontier peoples maintained a long tradition of horsemanship. These *auxilia* were organised as *quingenary alae* (with a strength of 512 men) or *milliary alae* (with a strength of 768 men).

Following the Flag

Under the early emperors, a legion or an auxiliary cohort would have many duties, from guarding granaries or post houses, to arresting dissidents, conducting patrols, overseeing some industrial activity and so on. Sometimes these duties took soldiers away from their home fort for weeks or months, but rarely were the troops posted outside of the province.

When an emperor was assembling an army for an assault on some foreign power, or if a frontier defence needed shoring up, he could call on those legions close at hand. He would also need to supplement this force with entire units from much further afield. Legio X Gemina, for example, was based in Germany but ordered to join emperor Trajan's invasion force for his attack on Dacia in AD 101. It did not return home but was relocated after the Dacian war to Pannonia. This legion was one of three in Pannonia that acclaimed Septimius Severus as emperor in 193. The uprooting of an entire legion to some distant battle-front, along with its staff, families and equipment was the way in which large-scale warfare was waged.

As legions became more entrenched within their home provinces and took up the burden of local frontier administration, it became a difficult matter to lift a legion out of its province. Instead a unit might be ordered to contribute a detachment of men for a particular campaign, a detachment that would return home once the war had ended. When the Jews rebelled against Roman rule in 132, for example, detachments from X Gemina marched east to reinforce the Roman army there. Later in 162, Lucius Verus, the co-emperor of Marcus Aurelius, took a detachment of the Gemina into Parthia, far to the east.

By the time of the Marcomannic Wars, this practice of ordering discrete bodies of men to fight for short periods in wars, before returning them to their forts, had become common. The Latin term for such a detachment was *vexillatio*, from the word for flag or banner: *vexillum*. These detachments marched under a temporary Roman military *vexillum*, which resembled a flag fluttering from a crossbar that was suspended from a central pole. It seems that the *vexillations* were brigaded together to form a more effective fighting force. They would either return home at war's end or, as happened to some *vexillations*, the troops would remain within the provinces they had fought in. Some, such as the *vexillatio equitum* Illyricorum, even became fully functioning units in their own right.

A typical combat detachment would normally be composed of one or more cohorts (*c.* 480 men) each of which could be separated from its parent legion easily and also take advantage of its internal six-century organisation. These centuries retained their own staff and had the ability to work independently. Together as a cohort the centurions commanding the centuries provided excellent leadership and an officer would be assigned to lead the detachment. Although his title was *praepositus*, he was most likely one of the five young tribunes (*tribuni angusticlavii*) that ordinarily performed staff functions within a typical legion. Assignment to lead a detachment could be great opportunity in the career of a young tribune, eager to make his mark.

Marcus Aurelius, the philosopher emperor, struggled to field enough soldiers using the system of *vexillations* alone. He was forced to create three new legions, Legio I, II and III Italica, but as tradition dictated, two of these were then settled into legionary bases on the frontier. Within five years these new legions were themselves sending out *vexillations* to places like Salonae, where detachments helped fortify the city against barbarian attacks.

There was no other easy way to mobilise troops for some new and troubling crisis. An emperor could either move entire legions, gambling that the frontier they protected would remain peaceful in their absence, or he could call on numerous individual detachments, which sometimes spread a legion out across more than one continent. During the crisis years of the third century attacks on the frontier became simultaneously more frequent and more widespread, the constant need for quick reaction forces necessitated the use of the *vexillation*. It could be mobilised rapidly and arrive at the frontier hot-spot to fight alongside other *vexillations* under a temporary commander. During the early third century *vexillations* sent to garrison frontier forts might expect to be deployed for up to three years. For those detachments engaged in field operations, however, a return home might be many more years away. Warfare in this chaotic century was almost constant and a full-strength *vexillation* was always needed somewhere along the frontier. A number of detachments spent so long operating in the field that they became, in effect, independent combat units.

Did Severus have an answer? He certainly moved legions around to help leverage the manpower he needed for his attacks on Parthia in 197 (and later in 208 on the north of Britannia). He also made use of *vexillations* to supplement his forces. Did his newly created Legio II Parthica, based in Italy, constitute a new type of military reserve? Although there is no evidence that Severus mobilised its troops to fight on the frontiers, his son, Antoninus, certainly did take large numbers of the legion eastwards to battle against the Parthians.

The New Reserve

The first Christian emperor of the Roman Empire, Constantine the Great, had at his command a mobile field army supplemented by entrenched frontier forces, or *limitanei*. While the *limitanei* garrisons slowed an enemy invasion but did not stop it, the field army was tasked with rushing to the region to prevent the barbarian force from penetrating any deeper into imperial territory. This was defence 'in depth' that planned to catch the enemy *after* it had crossed the frontier. It was the way of the future and a new system of military organisation that would be matched against the almost overwhelming barbarian invasions of the fourth and fifth centuries. Although Constantine ruled more than a hundred years after the time of Septimius Severus, it is possible to see the very start of this revolutionary new concept within Severus' own strategy.

Mobile armies, independent of fixed legions, are often seen as a feature of the Late Roman era, but the historian Michael Speidel noted that 'the field army is, in a sense, as old as the units stationed in Rome.' The Praetorian Guard had been Rome's garrison during the first two centuries of imperial rule but it was rarely deployed to a battle-front. Septimius Severus changed all that, in effect turning the Guard into Rome's first mobile (or 'imperial') field army. As we saw in chapter one, the emperor opened up recruitment to veterans of his Pannonian legions as a reward for loyal service. This also had the effect of elevating the Guard to the status of an elite fighting unit; members were all now battle-hardened veterans. One Praetorian proudly proclaimed on his tombstone that 'he had served in all the expeditions'.[4]

At a standing size of 10,000 soldiers and without the onerous administrative duties of units on the frontier, the Praetorian Guard had become the largest combat-ready force within the empire. It remained so throughout the third century and when paired with the new Severan unit, Legio II Parthica, became what was essentially the first effective imperial field army. The II Parthica was a regularly-sized legion of between 5,000 and 6,000 troops, but like the Guard, had no other duties. It was a lean fighting unit with an effective manpower greater than many other legions. Without other duties to tie it up, the II Parthica was always ready to march and to fight. Since it was always available, the II Parthica became the personal legion of the third century emperors and the unit's commander even became a member of the imperial retinue. In that sense, then, it was not a true independent field army but instead an imperial fighting unit that could provide a reserve of troops for other legions if necessary.

There were a number of other smaller units available at Rome that added to this new reserve, including one of the six Urban Cohorts of military police that patrolled the streets of the capital. Severus increased their membership which meant that a single cohort could contribute 1,500 soldiers to the army reserve. We know at least one cohort could be spared for combat duties after the presence of Urban Cohort XIV was recorded at Apamea in Syria, where it had fought alongside II Parthica.

A number of mounted units had been garrisoned in or around Rome for some time and these may also have bolstered the strength of the Severan army. Foremost among these cavalry units was the imperial guard cavalry, the *equites singulares* Augusti. Just as he had with the Urban Cohorts, Severus increased the membership of this elite force, doubling it from 1,000 to 2,000. To these he probably added many of the Moorish cavalry that had surrendered to Severus after the battle of Issus in 194. Together with the Mauri auxiliaries that already garrisoned Rome, this light cavalry force numbered around 2,000 individuals and it fought in battle with Antoninus, the eldest son of Severus who was to succeed him. Finally, the ancient writer Herodian recorded that Abgar IX, king of the defeated eastern kingdom Osrhoene, supplied Severus with a force of (horse?) archers for his invasion of Parthia in 197. These cavalrymen then joined the new imperial reserve and may have been garrisoned at Rome within the *castra peregrina*.[5]

Amassed together, the Severan reserve may have totalled around 21,500 soldiers, which provided Severus and his successors in the third century with an unprecedented combat force. *Vexillations* from other legions would then attach to this military core in order to create an expeditionary army able to invade Parthia or tackle the hostile German tribes on their own territory. The variation in troops or detachments assigned to the army depended of course on the location of the threat and the availability of manpower. Emperor Maximinus, for example, raised a unit of German cavalry whilst on campaign in the north, in order to augment his expeditionary force.

Cavalry was proving increasingly valuable. In wars of the past, emperors had time to assemble a large army by marching legions to a troubled province or weak frontier. Once the troops were assembled the invasion would be launched. Often this invasion was either one of retribution for some recent enemy attack, or more likely a pre-emptive strike against a rising power. Rome no longer had the time for this kind of strategy. What the third century crisis needed was mobility and a rapidly reacting force that could attempt to deal with constant raids and invasions on many different frontiers simultaneously. Having an army almost permanently in the field led personally by the emperor addressed this new demand, as did a recognition of the value of cavalry.

Soldier emperors had to lead from the front, which meant that Rome saw less and less of them. Meanwhile, well-fortified frontier cities that lay on good communication routes behind the embattled frontiers began to serve as *ad hoc* imperial centres. Colonia, Treverorum, Aquileia, Sirmium, Mediolanum, Vindobona ... all saw as much, if not more, of the emperor and his retinue than did Rome. Emperors could not leave this powerful military force in the hands of a trusted officer. This was to become a factor in any military deployment that had been relatively uncommon prior to the third century. Back in the first century AD the emperor Claudius, for example, had been able to leave the conquest of Britain to his general Aulus Plautius without fear that the general might suddenly turn the invasion force toward Rome.

The third century would illustrate time and time again that there were no longer any trusted men out there. A cycle of civil wars spanned the century as a long line of usurpers rose to seize the throne for themselves. Many emperors died violently and most of those deaths were the result of assassination. However, it was easier to gain power in the third century than it was to hold on to it; the reign of most of these emperors lasted for no more than a few months. The year 253, for example, saw the emperor Trebonianus Gallus murdered by his own troops as he prepared for battle against an usurper, Aemilius Aemilianus. Within months one of Aemilianus' own generals, Valerian, declared himself emperor and marched his armies south to seize the throne. Confrontation was avoided when Aemilianus' own army lynched him near Spoleto in October. While Gallus had reigned for just over two years, the rule of Aemilianus had lasted only eighty-eight days.

Cavalry Strike Force

It has long been thought that Valerian's son, Gallienus (reigned 260–268), created a powerful new, mobile and independent cavalry force that presaged the cavalry-dominated field armies of the fourth century. The new cavalry unit was named the *equites* Dalmatae and was recruited from the province of Dalmatia (located along the Adriatic coast) around 255. After fighting in Germany, it was based at Mediolanum (modern Milan) from where it was able to assist with the defence of the north Italian plain from an invasion by Alemanni or (more likely) pretenders to the throne.

With few reliable historical accounts from this period, evidence has to be gleaned from other fragmentary sources. The theory that Gallienius' cavalry unit formed Rome's first mobile field army was created by the eminent scholar Emil Ritterling in 1903, assisted by the work of the German numismatist Andreas Alföldi. Although once widely accepted, this theory has since been heavily criticised.[6] More likely, the *equites* Dalmatae as well as two units of mounted Moorish javelin men (the *equites* Mauri) and Osrhoene horse archers, simply served as supporting cavalry forces. There is little evidence that they were at all independent or enjoyed the command of a senior general; they acted, as cavalry had always acted, as a powerful skirmishing force. Their creation shows that cavalry was being used in greater numbers, but not that it was independent. The cavalry was most successful operating in conjunction with the infantry and as lightly armoured skirmishers they could not conduct the kinds of pitched battles that the heavy fourth century cavalry would later do at the battles of Adrianople, Chrysopolis and Campus Ardiensis. Cavalry in the fourth century would focus on heavily armoured cataphracts capable of shock attacks; nothing like that existed in any number during the third century.

The nature of the threats to Roman security throughout the third century necessitated the development of the available cavalry forces. Gallienus expanded his cavalry and organised it into new units of *equites* charged with the job of finding out the whereabouts of the enemy and goading it into the path of the main imperial army. These *equites* formations were wide-ranging, and enjoyed the freedom of an extended security force, yet did not constitute anything like a fourth century field army. Their existence, however, illustrates the strategic problems faced by emperors of the day. Threats were emerging continually, on all the major frontiers with greater and greater frequency, wars and incursions overlapping so much that the legions were being worn thin, propped up by *vexillations*, unable to move to another danger area for fear of leaving their own borders defenceless.

The Threat

From 226 onwards, the kingdom of Persia became a major thorn in the side of Rome, bringing death and destruction to the eastern provinces on an unprecedented scale. Meanwhile, renewed pressure from the German tribes from across the Rhine threatened the safety of the city of Rome itself. The third century was becoming a turbulent time of frontier crises and internal struggles ... and the *fracas* would be joined by the game-changers, the new people emerging from Russia: the Goths.

While the reasons behind the attacks on the frontiers are complex (and beyond the scope of this book) there is little doubt that Rome itself was in some measure to blame for their intensity. Ctesiphon, the Parthian capital, had been sacked twice in the second half of the 2nd century. Parthian military prestige and fighting ability had taken a hammering and had helped to create the perfect situation at home for Iranian 'regime change'.

Along the Rhine frontier Rome had sought to keep the peace for centuries through tribal dissension and the promotion of client chiefs. After the Marcomannic Wars these smaller tribes had begun to co-operate, finding a new strength and bargaining power when allied, rather than divided, as Rome would have wished. It was clear that as soon as some of the tribes entered into mutual confederations, the remaining tribes would hurry to do the same. Tribes familiar to the earlier emperors, like the Cherusci, for example, were subsumed within these new confederations, the Franks, Alemanni, Saxons and Burgundians. Along the Danube equally powerful tribal alliances were being created. It had been the intensity and duration of Rome's counter-attacks during the Marcomannic Wars that had forced the tribes to react in this way.

The Persians

> On the thirtieth day of the month of Xandikus of the year 239, the Persians descended upon us.
>
> Graffito from a house in Dura Europus.

Parthia had endured and thrived throughout the long rise of Rome. Heirs to the ancient Persian Empire of Darius and Xerxes and Alexander the Great, the Parthians had once been a tribe of steppe nomads that had crossed into Iran from the Kara Kum desert. The society ruled by the Parthian elite (the Arsacid dynasty) was feudal in nature, chieftains defending small regions who owed allegiance to provincial nobles who then looked to the king. All of these nobles fought on horseback during war, the richest as cataphracts, which were heavily armoured cavalrymen fighting with long spears, axes and swords and riding fully armoured horses. Poorer nobles fought as horse archers, a superb class of warrior that was fast moving, able to fight from a distance and that was difficult for the Roman legions to come to grips with. Cavalry defined the Parthian (and later Persian) method of waging war.

With no full time professional army available, military campaigns involved the mobilisation of local nobles who brought with them their own retinues, peasant levies and mercenary forces of hill-men and desert nomads. From time to time these nobles were at war with one another and civil war would split the feudal system, just as it had during Caracalla's reign.

The ancient Persians who had once ruled the Iranian plateau and beyond were once again in control of the region following Ardashir's victory over the Parthian king. This new dynasty, the Sassanian, would continue to challenge Rome in the east for another four centuries. Following the dynastic change would come a restoration of Persian noble families to power, a renewal of old Persian values, religion and art. Institutions like the unit of elite warriors, the Immortals, flickered into existence once again. In warfare the Persians inherited the Parthian feudal system and its reliance on cavalry as the main striking force. There is some suggestion of a professional and skilled military corps since the Persian army now begins to besiege enemy cities, something the Parthians could never attempt.

Of greatest worry to Rome was Persia's new found aggression. The Arsacid dynasty of the Parthians had been happy to maintain a status quo, defending against Roman attack when necessary and attacking in retaliation. The new Sassanian dynasty had in mind to restore the Persian Empire to its ancient glory and that meant sweeping Rome's eastern provinces away in order to replace them with Persian satrapies.

> (Ardashir) became a source if fear to us; for he was encamped with a large army against not Mesopotamia only but Syria also and boasted that he would win back everything that the ancient Persians had once held as far as the Grecian Sea.
>
> Dio Cassius 80.4

The Germans

'(a German) thinks it spiritless and slack to gain by sweat what he can buy with blood.'

Tacitus, *Germania* 14

Occupying the lands on the far bank of the river Rhine, lands of swamp and trackless forest, dwelt the German tribes. For the Romans, Germania represented a region that could not be conquered. Attempts had been made of course, emperor Augustus had wanted to push the frontier forward, from the river Rhine to the Elbe. His generals made war on the Germans, pushed the Roman forces deep into the dark forests until in AD 9 three legions were destroyed in the Teutoburg Forest. It was a military disaster from which Roman morale never recovered. The frontier was pulled back to the Rhine and (further east) to the Danube and there it remained. Raids, punitive expeditions and outpost forts would carry Roman power into this wild region, but it always remained 'beyond the frontier'.

German physique and martial spirit impressed and frightened the Romans. They were a tribal people, owing fealty to a local chief who led his warriors into battle to bring his tribe glory, wealth and security. His position was subject to change, the tribal assembly of elders (the *thing*) could always call for a new leader and so chiefs remained in power if they could secure success in war and the loyalty of their warriors. These chiefs or kings grew accustomed to allying together since large confederations could achieve more than one tribe alone. These super-tribes were the cause of the Marcomannic Wars that so threatened the empire in the 170s. Throughout the third century, German tribes like the Franks, Alemanni, Juthungi, Marcomanni, Quadi, Suebi, Burgundi, Chatti and others were poised to launch themselves against the Roman defences. Two factors drove the tribes onward, the first was booty and prestige that a king gained from raiding Roman territory and the second was the relentless pressure on tribal lands from tribes further east. The greatest threat from the German tribes was their relentless aggression. Year after year they would attack the Roman frontier, pushed onto the defences by the billiard ball-like repercussions caused by the movements of distant nomadic movements far away on the Asian steppe.

In battle the elite German warrior was a swordsman, protected by a shield but little, if any, armour. Poorer German fighting men were similarly unprotected but carried spears, javelins, axes or bows. Helmets and ringmail shirts were certainly available to members of the mounted nobility. From the second century onwards more and more Roman swords were being used by the tribes and a significant number have been found in ritual bog deposits, such as those at Vimose in Denmark and Thorsberg in Schleswig-Holstein, Germany.

The Sarmatians

The Marcomannic Wars heralded the very beginning of the barbarian attacks which resulted in the depredations of the third century and the eventual fall of the Western Roman Empire in the fifth. The term 'Marcomannic War' is a modern creation, those fighting it called the conflict the German and Sarmatian War (*bellum Germanicum et Sarmaticum*).[7]

The Sarmatians were a federation of horse-riding nomad tribes that had occupied the southern Russian plains for several centuries. By the reign of Marcus Aurelius several sub-tribes, including the Iazyges and Roxolani, had moved westwards into Europe and settled in the lower Danube valley. Although they had established farming communities, it seems the Sarmatians retained a semi-nomadic lifestyle. Ammianus Marcellinus writes that they: 'travel over very great distances chasing others or themselves turning their backs, being mounted on swift and obedient horses and leading one or sometimes two, so that changing may maintain the strength of their mounts and their vigour be renewed by alternate rests.'[8]

From the Danube region they joined with the German tribes in their attacks on Roman cities. Pressure from the southerly migration of east Germans (the Goths) moving south into the Black Sea region intensified the Sarmatian pressure on Rome. Sarmatian successes have been credited with the tactical innovation of the cataphract, where man and horse are completely covered in ring-mail or scale armour to create a heavy cavalry striking force.

An aristocratic warrior elite (the *argaragantes*) ruled the tribes, whilst the majority of the work was done by the serf-like *limigantes*. Tribes were nomadic, moving from place to place on horseback or on the covered steppe-wagons, the *kibitkas*; they were also warlike, structured according to client and vassal relationships, in a very similar way to the Germans. Powerful warlords could attract significant followers with smaller clans and sub-tribes eager to share in glory and gold. Continual warfare between the Sarmatian tribes and the Danubian legions of the late second century brought the two forces into close contact on a regular basis. There would be an inevitable exchange of fashion, weaponry and tactics because of this. It would not just be Romans that would emulate the expert horsemen of the Sarmatian tribes, the Goths too learnt much from these people.

The threat from the Roxolani and Iazyges came from their perfection of the heavy cavalryman, something relatively new to Roman warfare. A Sarmatian warrior noble wore a helmet and a coat of armour (either scale, ringmail or 'locked scale') that often covered his arms and legs. Not only that, but his horse was protected by a similarly armoured helmet (chamfron) and trapper. Equipped with a long and heavy two-handed lance, the rider could participate in a charge that would scatter light infantry or cavalry. This was an innovation that would later be perfected by the chivalric knights of the High Medieval period.

The Goths

From Scandinavia, centuries before the time of Septimius Severus, a number of east German tribes began a slow migration southward through Poland

and Russia which eventually brought them into conflict with the Sarmatian tribes and, ultimately, Rome. Goths and Vandals would eventually carve up the Western Roman Empire between them, but, in the third century they were settling in Dacia and Thrace on the northern banks of the river Danube. With much in common with German tribes like the Quadi and Alemanni, the Goths fielded swordsmen and heroic noble warriors in battle, supported by an army of levy farmers carrying spears, javelins and axes. Just like their cousins on the Rhine, the Goths were known for their ferocity in battle.

Although there were many similarities in language, house building and in the gods they worshipped, the Gothic and Vandal tribes had spent many years on the Russian plain rubbing shoulders with the Sarmatians. They and some of the German tribes involved in the Marcomannic Wars (such as the Quadi) adopted Sarmatian 'customs and arms'.[9] Weapons decorated with Sarmatian animal art became popular amongst warriors; nomadic sword pommels, some be-jewelled with red garnets, became highly prized.

It was the famous horse-skills of the Sarmatians, though, that the Goths took for themselves. Although the German tribes of the Rhine and Danube had always utilised cavalry, it was in the time-honoured fashion: an unarmoured horseman throwing javelins or equipped with a spear and shield ready to ride down fleeing infantry or harass a formation of swordsmen. Gothic formations, in contrast, typically had a greater proportion of horsemen and consequently were far more mobile. Still, the Gothic economy was metal-poor, few warriors wore armour or helmets and few wielded swords and many of the swords found in barbarian graves differed little from the Roman long-sword (*spatha*).[10]

In the third century the Goths reached the Black Sea coast and, determined to drive southward into rich Roman lands, they created an *ad hoc* naval force of commandeered ships to begin a campaign of piracy in the Aegean Sea (268). This was a shocking new development for the Roman military which had not seen seaborne raiding on this scale for centuries. The Aegean served as a highway that unfortunately brought the raiders deep into the vulnerable heart of the Roman Empire, the *mare Nostrum* ('Our Sea'). These audacious attacks, as well as the raids of the Alemanni, Juthungi and Marcomanni into Italy, profoundly affected the strategic thinking of the Roman hierarchy.

3

The Crisis Begins

'Despising our arms and contemptuous of the Roman reputation, [the Persian king] is attempting to overrun and destroy our imperial possessions. I first endeavoured by letters and persuasion to check his mad greed and his lust for the property of others. But the king, with barbarian arrogance, is unwilling to remain within his own boundaries and challenges us to battle. Let us not hesitate to accept his challenge.'

Alexander Severus speaking to the soldiers, Herodian 6.3

After having fought two civil wars and carried out two eastern invasions, it was not likely that Septimius Severus would settle down to a life of ease within Rome's imperial palace on the Palatine Hill. Imbued with a restless energy and eager to find some way in which he could occupy his two squabbling sons, he looked toward Britannia. There had been trouble in the north of that province and in 197 the Roman governor, Virius Lupus, had bought off the two largest tribes, the Caledonii and the Maetae. If Severus had wanted to respond with force then this blood money had to suffice since the emperor was busy in the east with his invasion of Parthia. By 207 the warriors of the Caledonii and Maetae were gathering for more raids into Roman territory. The new governor of Britannia dispatched an urgent request for help from Rome:

> ... the barbarians had risen and were overrunning the country, carrying off booty and causing great destruction ... for effective defence more troops or the presence of the emperor was necessary.
>
> Herodian III.14

In early 208 the emperor, the imperial family, a senatorial council, a host of courtiers and advisors as well the Praetorian Guard and *vexillations* from several legions crossed the Channel to arrive in Britain. While his youngest son Geta remained at the city of York to administer the province, Severus took the eldest son, Antoninus on the march with him. York became an imperial capital and it is likely that the commander of York's garrison, Legio VI Victrix, gave up his luxurious residence within the fort to serve as a temporary imperial palace. The legionary fortress at York served as the headquarters for the entire military zone of the north of England and was well connected to cities and ports further south, as well as forts on Hadrian's Wall.

As the army marched north it was accompanied by a fleet of transports that must have put in at Arbeia, a strategically located fort at South Shields on the mouth of the River Tyne. During the intense preparations for invasion the auxiliary fort had been enlarged and heavily modified. Whereas a typical fort would maintain a couple of granaries for the feeding of its 500-strong garrison, the Severan conversion boasted an incredible twenty-two granaries! Calculations show that up to 40,000 men could be fed from this supply base for up to three months. These supplies would be shipped along the Tyne to garrisons on the Wall and up the coast to feed and equip the Severan armies as they marched along the east coast of Scotland.

Severus waged two ferocious campaigns against the tribes north of Hadrian's Wall, first in 209 and again in 210. On one occasion, the ambitious (and ruthless) Antoninus made an attempt on his father's life, or so it appeared to witnesses. Both emperors (for Severus shared the throne with his son) were riding ahead of the army to parley with a group of Caledonii chiefs. When some of the officers saw Antoninus raise his sword as if to strike Severus, they gave a shout and alerted the emperor. Later, in private, he admonished his son, not for attempting to kill him, but for attempting it in front of the army!

On 4 February 211, Septimius Severus died following a prolonged illness. He was sixty-five. The battle-weary senator from North Africa left the empire in the hands of his two sons and their mother, Julia Domna. The brothers hastened to Rome with the imperial entourage and the army as soon as a peace treaty with the northern tribes had been arranged. By the end of the year Geta was also dead, murdered by the hand of Caracalla according to one account. He was successor to Septimius Severus and heir to the Roman Empire. Severus would be survived by a dynasty that would outlast him by a quarter of a century.

Caracalla: Son of Severus

> Rejoice, fellow-soldiers, for now I am in a position to do you favours." And before they heard the whole story [Antoninus] had stopped their mouths with so many and so great promises that they could neither think of nor say anything to show proper respect for the dead. "I am one of you," he said, "and it is because of you alone that I care to live in order that I may confer upon you many favours, for all the treasuries are yours." And he further said: "I pray to live with you, if possible, but if not, at any rate to die with you. For I do not fear death in any form, and it is my desire to end my days in warfare.
>
> Caracalla addressing the legions after he had murdered Geta, Dio Cassius 78.3.

The imperial dynasty that Severus founded was a little unconventional by the standards of Rome. Antoninus played the soldier just as his father had taught him. He marched with the soldiers on foot rather than travelling by carriage, he ate the legionary rations and, it is said, even ground his own flour with a hand-mill. Gaining the loyalty of the soldiers further he increased the pay of the troops again (costing the treasury a staggering seventy million sesterces) and led the legions into battle against the Germans. It was probably on this campaign in 213 that Antoniunus began wearing the long, hooded cloak of the locals. Called the *caracallus*, it earned him the nickname of Caracalla amongst the soldiers and commentators of the day. One of the most fascinating decrees of any emperor was made by Antoninus early on in his reign; he extended Roman citizenship to all free-men of the empire. Why? In doing so he was able to increase the tax base and he may have widened the obligation for public service. Nevertheless, this attempt to wring out more funds from the populace had other ramifications, not least was the unity that the people of the empire now enjoyed. Hispania and Syria, Gaul and Raetia ... all were put on an equal footing. The armies of Rome were also dramatically affected, if all soldiers were now citizens of Rome then the *auxilia* were now citizens and of equal social status to the men of the legions. It is unclear how this affected pay for the auxiliary units or if this changed how they were utilised.

Caracalla's wicked side soon emerged. He had already massacred perhaps as many as 20,000 people that he believed to be supporters of the murdered Geta. Following his war against the Germans, a leisurely tour of Dacia, Thrace and Asia Minor followed. His destination was Alexandria, site of Alexander the Great's tomb with whom the young emperor had come to increasingly identify. During his stay at the Egyptian city some incident occurred in 216 that enraged Caracalla, causing him to lure many of the city's youth to an ambush where they were massacred by his soldiers. Murder and mayhem spread to other parts of the city, thousands of unarmed civilians were massacred. It is likely that the Alexandrians were openly critical of the murder of Geta, an act which burdened the emperor with guilt and insecurity throughout his reign.

Antioch was to be the assembly point for an invasion of Parthia. Caracalla wished to lead the armies east just as his father, and his hero Alexander, had done. It was a great time to strike – a civil war had split apart the military forces of the Parthian empire. The legions crossed both the Euphrates and Tigris rivers to ravage and plunder the lands of the Parthians and they returned relatively unscathed. A second expedition against the Parthians was planned for the following year after the emperor had spent the winter at Edessa. He must have been in regular contact with his mother who had remained at Antioch.

Caracalla might have earned the trust of the legions but he remained vulnerable to conspiracy and assassination nevertheless. It took only one man to kill an emperor and that man was Julius Martialis, a member of the imperial bodyguard. According to the writer Herodian, Martialis wanted revenge for his brother who had been executed on an unproven charge. Cassius Dio claims that Martialis had been denied promotion to the centurionate and was bitter and angry about the decision. At the same time, Julia Domna had received a report that a plot had formed against her son and that Marcus Opellius Macrinus, the commander of the Praetorian Guard, was one of the ring-leaders. Fact? Gossip? Unfounded allegation?

On 8 April 217, Caracalla set out from Edessa to the city of Carrhae. Both Martialis and Macrinus, along with the imperial bodyguard, accompanied the emperor. It was after Caracalla had dismounted and dropped his breeches in order to relieve himself away from the road that Martialis stepped forward and cut him down. With a single sword thrust he was dead, and despite making an attempt to flee on horseback, the assassin was killed by a quick thinking member of the shocked bodyguard. The army cremated Antoninus and sent his ashes to Rome, within weeks his mother had followed her son to the grave, her ashes joining those of Caracalla and Severus within the Mausoleum of Hadrian on the banks of the Tiber.

An Unconventional Dynasty

> I will not describe the barbaric chants which [Elagabalus], together with his mother and grandmother, chanted to [the Syrian god], or the secret sacrifices that he offered to him, slaying boys and using charms, in fact actually shutting up alive in the god's temple a lion, a monkey, and a snake, and throwing in among them human genitals, and practising other unholy rites, while he invariably wore innumerable amulets.
>
> Dio Cassius 80.11

With no son of his own or any heir nominated to succeed him, Caracalla left the Roman Empire without an emperor. Perhaps Macrinus, the Guard commander, had been involved in the conspiracy but if so he waited three days before stepping forward. He turned to the troops who acclaimed him emperor on 11 April. By the autumn of 217 Macrinus had finished placing his own trusted men in positions of power, but he was unprepared for a counter-strike by the Parthians who had been building up their forces during the summer months. Following a tremendous battle close to the city of Nisibis, in Mesopotamia, the forces of Macrinus were forced to retreat. He paid for a Parthian peace in hard cash, a pay-off worth 200 million sesterces. The soldiers were less than impressed with their new emperor.

At this critical time in the east a young man was unveiled to the troops of Legio III Gallica stationed at Raphanaea, near Emesa. Only fourteen years-old, this 'False Antoninus' was actually Varius Avitus the son of Julia Soaemias and grandson of Julia Maesa (who was the sister of Julia Domna). Through this real blood connection and the rumour that Avitus was actually an illegitimate son of the dead Caracalla, the boy was acclaimed emperor by this rogue legion. It had declared against Macrinus which meant that civil war was in the offing. Despite a hasty distribution of money to the troops Macrinus could not stop other legions in the east from siding with Avitus (better known to history by the name of Elagabalus).

Legions loyal to both emperors clashed outside Antioch on 8 June 218 and the armies of Macrinus were defeated. In an attempt to flee into Europe he was captured and later executed. Why had the soldiers turned so fiercely upon their new emperor? In the first instance they had been forced into an ignominious climb-down by the Parthian king, in the second, Macrinus realising he could not hope to continue paying the huge wages agreed by Caracalla, reduced the wages of new recruits to Severan levels. As Cassius Dio observed, if this had been done in peace-time, when the legions were ensconced within their regular barracks, they would most likely have done nothing. After all, serving soldiers were to continue receiving the pay offered to them by Caracalla. With the legions now in the field in close proximity with one another and fearing further cuts once the war was at an end, they became at once suspicious, hostile and rebellious.

The reign of Macrinus, although short-lived, was an aberration, a gap in the Severan dynasty. Now, the politicking of Julia Domna's sister, Julia Maesa, was to ensure that the 'False Antoninus', the teenager Varius Avitus, would continue the bloodline. He would prove to be an unconventional Roman and perhaps the most bizarre and extraordinary emperor to ever don the purple. He had none of the abilities or qualities that the troops might admire; what had brought him to prominence was simply his blood relation to Septimius Severus, the legions' beloved soldier-emperor. If they thought he might be blessed with similar martial traits, they were wrong.

Firstly, history knows Avitus as Elagabalus which was the name of his god, for the youth grew up at Emesa in Syria and served as the hereditary high priest of the god Elagabal. When he arrived at Rome in 219 Elagabalus was accompanied by his family as well as a sacred black stone from the temple at Emesa. This stone was the god of the Emesenes and the emperor had it installed within a purpose-built temple on the Palatine Hill. It would not stop there; Elagabal was to have sovereignty over all Roman gods, and take the hand in marriage of the virgin goddess Pallas. As part of this arrangement the boy emperor planned to wed one of the sacred Vestal Virgins. Of course this meddling with the religion of the Roman state scandalised Roman society. They were just as shocked at his sexual adventures. Married to at least three wives in three years, he was reputed to have had many other affairs both with women and men. Most scandalous of all, Elagabalus began to frequent Rome's brothels dressed as a woman and in this guise he 'married' his Carian slave boy.

Without the careful administration of affairs by his Syrian kinsfolk, this strange young man would not have lasted his first year in office. As it was his reign spanned four years. There was serious disapproval. Both Legio IV and Legio III Gallica, which had proclaimed him emperor, attempted to raise a pretender to the throne without success. Nevertheless the sour mood of the soldiers was now a cause for great concern. In 221 the court followers, family and supporters of Elagabalus persuaded him to adopt one of his own cousins, Bassianus Alexianus, as his son and heir. Only thirteen years-old, this young man would inherit the empire within the year and take the name of Alexander Severus.

The two youths were soon at odds, supported by their partisan families. Elagabalus was backed by his mother Julia Soaemias, Alexander Severus by his mother Julia Mamaea and grandmother Julia Maesa. The new upstart had the Praetorian Guard's approval and this fact enraged Elagabalus in 222 when he heard them shout Alexander Severus' name during a visit to the Praetorian camp. [1] His order for the arrest of the offenders pushed the Praetorians too far and they killed him on the spot, disposing of the body in the traditional Roman way. Like any common criminal the exotic eastern priest and emperor of Rome was beheaded and thrown unceremoniously into the River Tiber.

Rome probably braced itself for the reign of another out-of-control eastern youth, but Alexander Severus provided the empire with some much needed stability. Ancient historians look on him with favour and admiration, although it must be remembered that many decisions were being made in his name by his mother, Julia Mamaea and her supporters. This was no secret, she ruled jointly with her son and by 227 was styling herself *mater augusti et castrorum et senatus et patriae* (mother of the emperor, the garrisons, the senate and the homeland). Mistakes made by her sister Julia Soaemis with Elagabalus would not be repeated. The empress established a council of senators to advise her and kept strict control over her son's private life. The gods of Rome were returned to their rightful place and the sacred black stone was shipped back to Syria.

Despite lacking the excesses of his cousin's previous reign, all was not peace and harmony. The Praetorian Guard still flexed its muscles when the mood called for it. In 223 or early 224 they assassinated their own commander, Domitius Ulpianus, for his execution of two of their own officers. Prior to that some of the Praetorians had argued bitterly with the Roman populace and took part in three days of street-fighting with many casualties on both sides.

At this time an event occurred in the east that would have terrible repercussions for the Roman Empire and its citizens for the next fifty years. The Parthian kingdom had been in decline for some decades and was finally overthrown by the once powerful Persians. The Persian king, Ardashir, defeated the Parthian king Artabanus in April 224. Two years later he had seized control of Parthia and re-established a Persian Empire that consciously looked back to the Persian glories of the past, when its soldiers dictated Greek policy in the west and commanded loyalty from Indian kings in the east.

In 230 Ardashir led his Persian army into northern Mesopotamia to reclaim those territories lost in 197 to Septimius Severus. The emperor had to respond with a military expedition despite his youth and his inexperience of military matters – the direct aggression of the new Persian regime had to be checked. Detachments of troops from the Danube armies joined Legio II Parthica and the Praetorian Guard to march east to Antioch in the summer of 231. Here preparations for a counter-attack were interrupted by a mutiny. Alexander had punished soldiers from Legio II Traiana, who had marched up from Egypt to join the expedition, for using the baths and brothels throughout the city. With a combination of threats and admonishment he brow-beat the legion and convinced them to abandon their mutiny. The Persian campaign of 232 was not decisive and both sides suffered large numbers of casualties. Although the Persian king made no more attacks on Roman territories during Alexander's reign, the military reputation of the young emperor had suffered and the morale of the legions had taken a blow.

No sooner had the emperor returned to Rome to celebrate his 'victory' over the Persians than reports were received that German tribes had breached the Rhine frontier and were laying waste to Roman territories. Alexander led an expedition across the Rhine in 234 but instead of bringing the tribes to battle he made arrangements to pay them off. Politically it may have been a wise move but the soldiers were incensed at such appeasement, they had turned on the emperor Macrinus in 217 when he had paid for peace with the Parthians.

The soldiers were grumbling. After a massacre of Roman troops and the resulting retreat from Persia followed by an unprosecuted war against the Germans, they could see neither glory nor gold at the hands of Alexander. Camp chatter ridiculed him as a 'mummy's boy' and too timid to fight. In 235 some of them decided to offer the throne to one of their own officers, Gaius Julius Verus Maximinus. On the parade ground they threw a purple cloak around his shoulders and despite his protests (real or feigned) he was forced to accept. It is doubtful that this came as a shock to Maximinus, he had almost certainly engineered the coup himself, acting on the grievances of his men. The rebel troops hastened from their base at Mainz to Bretzenheim where the emperor was encamped. Here the rest of the army rallied behind Maximinus, proclaiming him emperor and sending a party of centurions into the imperial tent to murder the weeping Alexander along with his mother, Julia Mamaea.

So ended the dynasty of Septimius Severus. Alexander enjoyed a blood-tie to his illustrious forebear and retained his name, yet he had never benefited from that piece of advice that the old man had whispered into his sons' ears: 'agree with each other, give money to the soldiers, and scorn all other men.'

Despite showing largesse to his surviving legions after their retreat from Persia in 232, Alexander failed to curry favour with the soldiers in the way that Severus or Caracalla had done. Like it or not, this was the cold, hard reality of politics now; the armies of Rome had to be flattered, bribed, cajoled and honoured. Maximinus was one of them, he had started from the very bottom and worked his way up to become emperor. He was a soldier to the core, not an senator, or a wealthy merchant, a priest or an imperial heir... he had joined the military in Thracian Moesia as an auxiliary cavalryman, lower in status even than a legionary recruit.

The first act of Maximinus on gaining the throne was to double the soldiers' rations, revoke all outstanding sentences and punishments and promise his legions lavish financial rewards.

Severus' unconventional dynasty had stumbled and fallen. Maximinus, the common soldier, represented the very outcome Septimius Severus had worked so hard to avoid during his eighteen years in power. A reluctance to give the legions what they wanted had first provoked them to find a candidate who would. In Maximinus they had even done away with that step, rather than select a willing candidate they had simply elevated one of their own. It had never been done before, the Thracian trooper was the most low-born of all emperors, but he was someone with whom the legions could identify and who understood their wants and needs. Surely in an empire ruled by the common soldiery, a common soldier would go far?

The Senate Responds

> I think it my duty to set down in writing the decree of the senate in which the Gordians were declared emperors and Maximinus a public enemy... the consul cried: "Maximinus is our enemy; the gods shall now bring it to pass that he may now cease to be, and that we with joyful hearts may enjoy the happy sagacity of the Elder Gordian, and the intrepid virtue of [his son, the Younger Gordian]."
>
> Historia Augusta, *The Three Gordians 11*

It was unlikely that Maximinus would immediately march for Rome to take up residence with the imperial palace. In fact he never stepped foot in Rome during his entire reign. In the summer of 235 he led the legions across the Rhine to make war on German tribes in the Württemberg and Taunus regions, for the next two years he led expeditions into the Danube region where he fought the Sarmatians. These wars were costly and Maximinus funded them through the confiscation of private property in Italy and through blatant extortion of the wealthy. This had been done before but rarely on such a scale; the soldier emperor went further, however, even exacting funds by reducing the corn dole of the urban poor.

Within three years Maximinus' plundering of the empire had created a significant amount of resistance from all strata of society. The spark of resistance finally flared up in Africa Proconsularis, a wealthy province that did not suffer the kind of frontier problems that justified the exorbitant new taxes. A gathering of locals at Thysdrus (modern El Djem) ambushed the finance officer and killed him. There were no legions within the province and so the locals approached the governor, an eighty-year-old senator named Marcus Antonius Gordianus Sempronianus and hailed him as emperor. When Rome's senate heard the news it eagerly recognised him, Gordian was one of their own and could hopefully restore the balance of authority. At the provincial capital of Carthage, Gordian received the news that the senate had given both he and his 42 year-old son (Gordian II) the title of Augustus. Both were now emperors.

Events moved quickly. Maximinus heard the news but before he could reach Rome to re-establish his claim on the imperial title, the governor of Numidia (adjacent to Africa Proconsularis) marched on Carthage with Legio III Augusta. In the fighting Gordian II was killed and the elder Gordian committed suicide. Had the attempt of the senate to take back its legitimacy and power been snuffed out before it had even begun? It could not afford to give up now, Maximinus would show absolutely no mercy to the senators if he successfully reached the capital. In desperation they elected two new emperors, Decius Caelius Calvinus Balbinus who would administer the state and Marcus Clodius Pupienus Maximus who would be responsible for defence. Both men were old, perhaps in their sixties or seventies and to appease the Roman mob they invited the thirteen year-old grandson of the elder Gordian (Gordian III) to join them as a junior emperor, a Caesar.

Maximinus arrived in northern Italy with his legions and, finding the city of Aquileia opposed to him, began a siege. For weeks the siege dragged on until, in April 238, some of Maximinus' troops that were normally garrisoned in Italy (soldiers of the Praetorian Guard and Legio II Parthica are said to have been involved) turned on their emperor, broke into his tent and murdered him.

It seemed the senate had won out over the armies of Rome at last, but it was not to be. The Praetorians did not like the idea of serving emperors chosen by the senate and in May they dragged the two elderly emperors through the streets back to the Praetorian camp where they were executed. Perhaps surprisingly, the Guard elevated the young Gordian III to the throne in their place. Like Elagabalus and Alexander Severus, Gordian was a mere boy and would be manipulated by his advisors, including both his mother and by the commander of the Guard, Gaius Furius Timesitheus.

War loomed. Almost every emperor of the third century faced the prospect of defending his empire in person and Gordian III was no exception. The

Persian kingdom had a new and dynamic king, Shapur, who was eager to begin hostilities with Rome. Timesitheus organised the military expedition and in 243 accompanied the emperor eastwards into Syria. The campaign was a success, a victory at the battle of Rhesaina in northern Mesopotamia allowed the recapture of the crucial caravan cities Nisibis and Carrhae.

Gordian, now nineteen years-old, could not celebrate his victory for long. Timesitheus died of natural causes while on campaign and with his guardian out of the picture, senior officers began to cause trouble for the young emperor. Military set-backs and supply problems were blamed on Gordian and because of this he was talked into accepting a regent, an officer called Marcus Julius Philippus (known to history as Philip 'the Arab'). As pressure increased Gordian decided to call the army's bluff. At Circesium on the Euphrates river he called the soldiers together and asked them to choose between Philip and himself. Tragically for the nineteen year-old, they chose Philip. Gordian was killed by the men who had acclaimed him emperor six years earlier, they buried him near Circesium and erected a monument there in his name. When the emperor Julian passed that way more than a hundred years later, he made sacrifice to the memory of the young Gordian who had succumbed to 'treacherous murder'.[2]

It was April 248, the 1000th anniversary of Rome's foundation and of course there were celebrations in Rome, complete with a spectacular series of gladiatorial games. This should have been the high-point of Roman history, a celebration of the empire's thousand-year rise to glory and dominance. However, the fate of Rome looked desperate indeed from the perspective of the new emperor Philip. Goths, a new and warlike group of northern tribes, had crossed the Danube in force and tried to take the Moesian city of Marcianopolis (modern Devnya). Usurpers challenged Philip throughout his five year reign. The commander of the Moesian and Pannonian armies declared himself emperor but was cut down by his own soldiers, the eastern officer Iotapianus was proclaimed emperor, as was Silbannacus and Sponsianus, military leaders on the Rhine and Danube frontiers respectively.

Although Philip was able, more by luck than strategy, to quell these rebellions, it was almost inevitable that he would succumb to some other rival. It was Quintus Decius Valerinus who would turn on the emperor and seize the throne for himself. Decius had been dispatched to govern the troubled provinces of Moesia and Pannonia; after he had successfully fought the Gothic invaders, he marched on Rome. In September or October 249, Philip contested this uprising. The two armies met at Beroea in Macedonia where Philip was defeated and killed.

Decius was not a military man, a common soldier in the mould of Maximinus or Philip, he was a senator from a distinguished family who had been appointed governor in the time-honoured tradition. He returned to Rome and spent some time there, co-ordinating several building projects and repairs but the frontiers continued to call ... In 250 he led legions against the Goths who had once again crossed the Danube into Roman territory. Fierce fighting followed and in June 251 the unthinkable occurred, Decius emperor of Rome was killed in battle. This was unprecedented, although, when one considers how much time each emperor was having to spend in the field, it was inevitable. Decius had been an 'old-style' emperor if one looks as far back as Septimius Severus, himself a senator and provincial governor with an eye to the main chance. Had he lived he may have returned to the senate its traditional authority, yet even Decius in his short year-and-a-half reign, faced two usurpers.

Barbarian attacks and the challenges of ambitious usurpers seemed to be increasing at break-neck speed, one fuelling the other. Why? To combat new and powerful threats to the integrity of the empire, such as the Goths, the Sarmatians and the Persians, for example, large Roman armies needed to be assembled to defeat them. If armies were not led by the emperor in person then the risk was great that a successful general would capitalise on his soldiers' victories to carry him to Rome. Legions liked to win and they liked to back winners. As soon as the precedent had been set, any governor lucky in war recognised that he had a good chance of seizing the throne. Severus had done it, so had Philip, Macrinus and Maximinus the Thracian. It had been done. It could be done again.

When the emperor was in the field, victory reflected glory upon him. Defeat or intransigence could be fatal. An emperor who did not deliver victory was quickly dispatched and so became the fate of Macrinus, the young Alexander Severus and Gordian III. The dilemma of a third century emperor was either to lead his legions in person and risk defeat and dethronement, or to rely on a trusted lieutenant who, if he achieved a real victory on the frontier, would almost certainly turn around and take the throne. With attacks across the border becoming more frequent and of greater intensity, it was now impossible for the emperor to plug all of the leaks in person, the crisis had reached a point where reliance on subordinates was now mandatory.

A replacement for Decius was quickly found. The soldiers took a shine to Trebonianus Gallus, the governor of Upper Moesia who had played an important role within Decius' war against the Goths. Gallus wanted to consolidate his authority by returning to Rome and in doing so had to make an unhappy peace with the Goths, leaving in their grasp many Roman hostages kidnapped by them for later ransom. He found Rome wracked by plague, this was not new to Rome since outbreaks had occurred on and off since the days of Marcus Aurelius. Both the senate and the people of Rome warmed to their new emperor but events within Rome were merely a side-show compared to the dramatic events occurring on the frontiers. Shapur, king of kings, had launched a new offensive in the east. In 252 his army defeated the eastern legions at Barbalissos, then marched onwards to overrun the Roman province of Syria. The populace city of Antioch, which served as Rome's capital in the east, was captured by Shapur's forces in 253.

Simultaneously the Goths reneged on their agreement with Gallus and began a series of attacks on Roman territory. Gallus' own replacement as governor of Upper Moesia, Aemilius Aemilianus, led the legions under his command into battle against the Gothic tribes with great success. The legions, flushed with victory, proclaimed him emperor and the governor (now emperor) marched on Rome. Gallus mustered an army with which to defend Italy and marched out to meet Aemilianus. He had gotten only 75 km north of Rome when the soldiers within Gallus' own army rebelled and murdered him, handing the empire to Aemilianus without a fight.

Aemilius Aemilianus, governor of Upper Moesia and an ex-consul of Rome, received the support of the senate. He promised to vanquish the invaders in the north and the east and hand the civil administration of the empire to the wisdom of the senate. Unfortunately, although he might have had big plans he had only four months in which to put them into practice. Trebonianus Gallus had called for reinforcements for his defence of Italy but those troops did not arrive in time. Their commander, the governor of the provinces of Noricum and Raetia, was Publius Licinius Valerianus. After Gallus' troops had murdered their emperor and joined with Aemilianus, Valerian's legions proclaimed their own general as emperor. Their eventual arrival into Italy behind the usurper Valerian caused Aemilianus' troops to desert. He was murdered at Spoleto in October 253 leaving Valerian free to enter Rome as the next emperor.[3]

We must presume that the senate was pleased to ratify the position of Valerian as emperor. He was one of their own after all, a senator who had served as consul and *princeps senatus* (an office similar to chairman) as well as provincial governor. The senate also accepted his son and colleague, Publius Licinius Egnatius Gallienus, as Augustus or co-ruler rather than just as Caesar. It seemed from the beginning of his rather colourful reign that Valerian realised the necessity of sharing power equally with his son. Valerian was also quick to divide their efforts geographically with Gallienus put in charge of the western half of the empire while Valerian himself concentrated on the eastern half.

These two emperors would come face to face with a series of monumental threats to the Roman Empire. During their desperate reigns the foreign forces ranged outside the empire, as well as the traitors conspiring within, pushed the empire to the brink of disaster. An overwhelming catastrophe was approaching that would have repercussions not only for the rest of Roman history but also for the history of Medieval Europe.

4

Appearance of The Soldiers

'[Severus] had incidentally ruined the youth of Italy ... filling the city with a throng of motley soldiers most savage in appearance, most terrifying in speech and most boorish in conversation.'

Dio Cassius 75.2

The third century and the troubled years of the second that preceded it, had a massive transformative effect on the legions and the soldiers within them. It was not just strategy, organisation, weaponry and armour that changed but also the way in which the soldiers dressed. This may seem like a minor point in an analysis of military change and its causes. In fact a study of military fashion within the barracks and on the parade ground can help us identify some of the sources of change. If you could stand a legionary from AD 100 next to one from AD 250 as they might be dressed around the fortress, the differences would be striking, indeed there would be few, if any, points of comparison. A 21st century observer might need some convincing that the third century soldier was in fact Roman! Partly this is due to representations of what a Roman soldier should look like in modern movies and TV programmes, but it is also due to the fact, as the quote at the start of this chapter illustrates, that the soldiers really were taking on a very 'un-Roman' appearance.

When Septimius Severus brought his armies into Rome in 193 the populace was shocked by their appearance. It is generally thought that this, along with their 'savage speech', indicates an adoption of barbarian dress. The citizens of Rome normally had little direct contact with the common soldier. Generals were forbidden to bring troops into Rome and the only military presence on the streets, the elite Praetorian Guard (which spent little time away from Rome) retained the traditional Roman garb familiar to the citizenry. If Romans wished to remind themselves of what one of the empire's glorious defenders looked like, they only had to look upon the magnificent triumphal carvings of Rome. Trajan's Column (AD 113) and the later Column of Marcus Aurelius (AD 180–193) provided detailed images of Roman soldiers on the march, in battle, carrying out executions, constructing forts and so on. But were they accurate?

In many ways the Column of Trajan does give a fairly accurate representation of the legionary of that era. The Column of Marcus Aurelius, however, is modelled on that of Trajan. The soldiers depicted do not match the emerging appearance of the Danube garrisons. Although there are some contemporary details, overall the carvings are formulaic, harking back to Trajan's Column and beyond.

The Roman Soldier in AD 100

Prior to the Marcomannic Wars then, before fashions began to change, what did the Roman soldier wear? Standard attire for any Roman male was the tunic, essentially a rectangle of thin wool folded over to make a square. When sewn up the sides, leaving holes at the top for the arms and with a slit cut along the fold for the head, it could not be a simpler garment to manufacture. Tunics were often very baggy and so were belted at the waist. While civilians used cord or fabric belts, legionaries lavished their pay on heavy leather belts decorated with metal plates and fastened with attractive metal buckles. Often an apron of leather strips, each one decorated with ornamental bronze discs, would hang from the front of the soldier's belt. The metalwork on his belt was a badge of status for a soldier off-duty, and the apron, jingling as he walked, emphasised this status, signalling to common folk, 'get out of my way, I am an agent of the emperor, with powers to detain, arrest and punish'.

Tunic colour varied amongst civilians as it may have amongst the troops also. However, a large body of evidence suggests that there were two main colours in use, a white tunic for everyday wear around the fort, on parade, off-duty, etc. and a red tunic worn when going to war.[1]

Trousers were certainly not worn, as a rule, being considered thoroughly barbaric and un-Roman. Most of the enemies of Rome wore trousers, whether they were from Britain, Germany, Dacia or Parthia. Barbarians recruited into the auxiliary cohorts retained their love of trousers, but it was not catching on within the legions. On his feet a soldier wore strong open-work, leather boots called *caligae* that were reinforced with iron hobnails. Protection from the elements and as a fashion accessory in its own right, troops wore one of two types of cloak; the first was called the *sagum* and was a rectangle of coarse wool, left undyed. The second was a semi-circular cape known as a *paenula* which included a hood. Both were popular, the *paenula* more so during the reign of Emperor Trajan.

When armed for war, the legionary donned an armour shirt, either of iron ringmail or bronze scale, or he wore *lorica segmentata*, the modern name for armour composed of curved strips of iron sheet. This is the type of armoured protection most commonly associated with Roman soldiers today. Typically he carried a large, rectangular, curved shield in his left hand into which he could lean and achieve a good measure of protection. In his right he wielded the *gladius*, a straight shortsword designed for fast thrusting attacks to an enemy's lower torso. When not in use it was stored in a decorated scabbard that hung from a baldric over the shoulder. It was once thought that common soldiers wore the *gladius* on their right side and centurions wore them on the left. Although this may have been a trend, there was in actual fact no hard and fast rule.[2]

The common helmets of Trajan's day were the Imperial-Gallic and Imperial-Italic types. Both were similar in construction and appearance, with an open face, large cheek-guards, a projecting brow guard and a wide projecting plate at the rear to protect the neck. An attachment on the crown enabled a crest to be fitted, perhaps to be worn on ceremonial occasions.

The *Dalmatic* Tunic

When Belgian archaeologists excavated the ancient Syrian city of Apamea they discovered seventy-six tombstones built into the fabric of the city's defences. Most of these grave stones had been ripped out of a nearby military cemetery and belonged to members of Legio II Parthica, the legion established by Severus that was normally garrisoned at Rome. Those that could be dated came from the early third century, specifically from the campaigns of Caracalla, Alexander Severus and Gordian III. Evidently the legionaries of this crack unit spent the winter months at Apamea, before returning to battle the Persians in springtime.

Besides a host of organisational details, the grave slabs offer a detailed illustration of the appearance of these soldiers. None are armoured; the legionaries wear tunics and belts, and swords hang from baldrics. The tunics were known as *dalmatica*, they were a new design, long sleeved with narrow cuffs. Not only that, but the soldiers are also depicted wearing trousers. Both of these items of clothing are associated with the barbarians. Throughout the third century more sculptural evidence, as well as a number of wall paintings, show that the fashion for long sleeved tunics had reached all units and all ranks. From the lowliest new recruits to seasoned veterans, from centurions and legionary commanders to even the emperor himself, all wore the same style of tunic, complemented with a pair of trousers and boots.

Where depictions of the tunic give some idea of colour, they appear as white or off-white. Many include decoration in the form of two narrow, coloured stripes running from the neck down across the chest (*clavii*), these lines often terminate in decorative arrowhead shapes. Similar stripes begin to appear at the wrist, which is always shown tight-fitting. In the latter half of the century legionaries may have had their tunics decorated with roundels or small geometric and animal motifs of the kind found in subsequent centuries. The practice was certainly begun by AD 300. A decorated fabric roundel was found within a tomb at Palmyra and may belong to the late third century. Even when

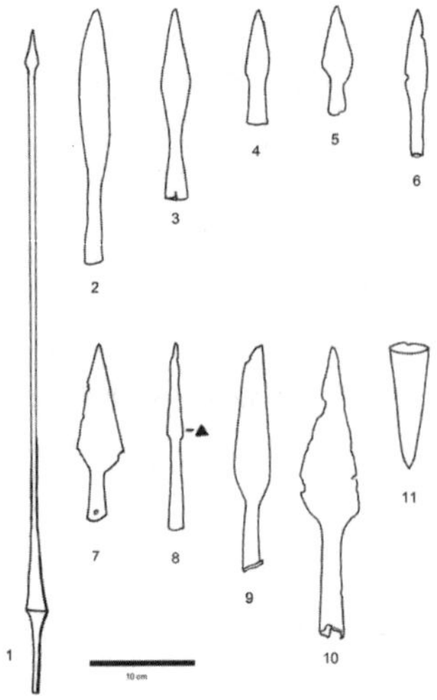

Third Century Spears. A range of Roman spearheads, and a spear butt (11) from the Third Century: 1 Saalburg; 2 Buch; 3 Künzing; 4-6 Saalburg; 7 Osterburken; 8 Künzing; 9 Osterburken; 10 Saalburg; 11 Osterburken (*after M. Daniels*)

some tunics were made of un-dyed linen, the fabric decoration (*clavii*, roundels and motifs) were always of wool, which takes dye more effectively than linen.

Fragments of some of these *dalmatic* tunics have been found at the ruined Roman city of Dura Europus in Syria. Others, including many in excellent condition, come from Egypt and date from the sixth and seventh centuries. These later Byzantine tunics show a clear lineage through from the third century and give us a good idea of their general appearance. One Dura tunic in particular was found in good condition. It was of white wool decorated with two purple stripes on each sleeve and two *clavii* descending from the shoulders. Although it closely resembles tunics seen on frescoes that were also found at the desert city, this example may have belonged to a child.

Since it represents one of the greatest changes in the appearance of the third century legionary, the important question to ask is: where did the influence for wearing long-sleeved tunics come from? Although we may never know for sure we can certainly narrow down the source of the influence from contact with either the Parthians or the Germanic tribes. This is a question we shall return to later on.

Trousers

The adoption of *dalmatic* tunics by the army was accompanied by a form of footed trouser that resembled medieval hose with integral feet, and they were quite tight fitting. We can assume that both tunic and trousers originated from the same place at the same time. Short, calf-length trousers (*bracae*) had certainly been seen within the ranks before 200; both legionaries and auxiliaries are shown wearing *bracae* on sculptural monuments from the Dacian Wars.[3] It is thought that auxiliary cavalrymen had originally adopted them but that the fashion spread first to the auxiliary infantry and later to the men of the legions.

From the reign of Septimius Severus until the end of the Roman era, it was a new style of full-length trousers that gained popularity with the military. Here we can be pretty certain that the fashion originated within the northern tribes since two pairs of these trousers have been recovered from the Thorsberg bog in Germany. Dated to the third or fourth century, these woollen trousers are fitted with integral 'feet' and exactly match trousers depicted in a fourth century Roman tomb painting from Silistra in Bulgaria. It is likely that the trousers of the third century legionaries also included this feature.[4]

Analysis of a well-preserved fresco from Dura Europus depicts the tribune Terentius leading his soldiers in worship (*see* Colour Plate 15). We can see that the colours of the various tight-fitting trousers on display appear to be either grey, dark blue or reddish-grey. Those worn by soldiers depicted in the fourth century Piazza Armerina mosaics from Sicily were certainly grey in colour, suggesting that the wool used was probably undyed.

Other than long trousers, soldiers may instead have worn leg-wraps, either rectangles of cloth wrapped around the lower leg and tied in place, or long, thin ribbons of fabric wrapped around the leg just as puttees were used by ground troops in the First World War. Leg protection like this had been typically worn by peasants or huntsmen for some time and may have been worn by soldiers during cold weather. An example of a leg-wrap was excavated at Sogaard's Moss in Denmark. Surprisingly the archaeologists were able to suggest a colour for the woollen cloth (blue), they also found part of the owner's leg still bound up inside the wrap! The puttee style of leg wrapping (*fascia*) was a recent third century innovation; it involved a single piece of dark cloth being wrapped around the leg in a bold inverted-V or herringbone pattern. While the huntsmen shown in the mosaics at Piazza Armerina wear *fascia* instead of trousers, it seem likely that

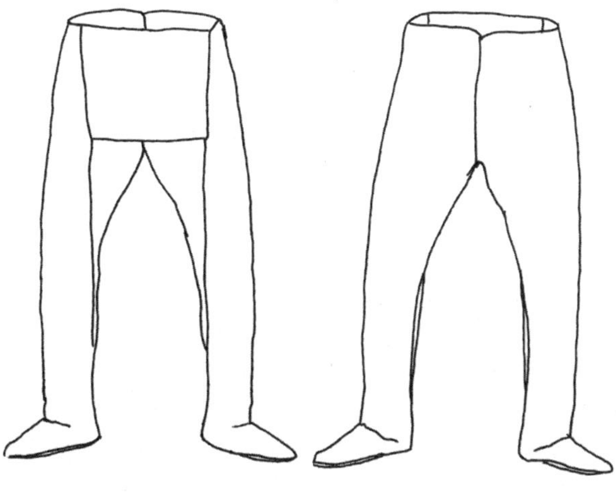

Footed trousers from Thorsberg. (*after Graham Sumner*)

both could be worn at the same time. According to the Historia Augusta, the emperor Alexander Severus 'always wore *fascia* on his legs and he wore white trousers, not scarlet ones, as had formerly been the custom.'[5]

The Boots

While the first century soldier campaigned across Europe in a pair of *caligae*, open leather boots that superficially resembling sandals, the late second and third century soldier enjoyed the benefit of *calcei*.[6] These were closed boots, very similar to modern walking boots, with the inclusion of a hob-nailed sole and leather laces. In some types these laces were simply long, thin extensions of the upper, threaded through cut-outs in the leather. There was no 'imperial issue' military boot akin to the British Army's Combat Assault Boot, yet the closed boot with integral laces is found as far apart as Usk and Saalburg in the west and Syria in the east. This added to the increasingly 'uniform look' of Roman troops during the third century.

There may well have been a preferred pattern in use by the Roman army, but local variations abounded. In fact the closed ankle boot, with its thick sole and toe protection, had been popular with the poorer segments of society, such as labourers and farmers, for some time. Its durability was no doubt recognised by Roman troops (who, like all soldiers in all eras, had good reason to obsess about their foot-wear).

Some of the cobbling techniques pre-figured medieval shoe-making practises, including the use of a sewn construction and butted side-seams. Some traditional Roman techniques continued however, such as the preference for attractive openwork cut-outs in the leather upper.

Socks (*udones*) may not normally be associated with Roman dress but were certainly worn. A writing tablet found at Vindolanda, in northern Britain, makes a request for a pair of socks.[7]

In addition, a child's sock was found on the site, made up of woollen cloth. Both the sock and the tablet are dated to the early second century, yet it is clear that socks are being depicted on some later, third century, military tombstones.

The Belt

A belt fastening can often date a military sculpture or a grave deposit, whereas something more utilitarian, like a spearhead or ringmail shirt, cannot. Throughout Roman history belts have been at the cutting edge of fashion, as a mark of military status and an obvious display of personal wealth. The third century was no different; for the entire period one type of distinctive belt buckle dominates the record. Being seen first on the II Parthican grave stones of Apamea, it was in the form of a bronze ring, through which two ends of a leather belt fed into and turned back on themselves. Studs are sometimes depicted, which fix the leather returns in place, and examples of these mushroom studs have been recovered from many military sites. There were a number of variations on the ring buckle, including openwork frame buckles, some with integral studs and other designs with loops and tongues that resemble traditional Roman (as well as modern) belt buckles. However, the ring buckle predominated.

Although the excavation of a simple bronze belt ring does not tell us anything about how it was actually worn, it is the wonderfully detailed tombstones of long dead legionaries that fill that gap. Carved with hammer and chisel and depicting the dead man in his daily clothing, these monuments were often erected at the instigation of grieving wives. It is fascinating to see the folds of their clothing, the weapons that they used and in some cases the stance they must have adopted in life. Aurelius Surus, trumpet player of Legio I Adiutrix is depicted cradling his beloved military trumpet in the crook of his left arm; Damianus, a *beneficarius* (military policeman) from Alexandria in Egypt, fiddles nervously with the loose ends of his belt. Artefacts lifted from the soil are given life by these sculptural testaments.

Two prevailing belt fashions seem to dominate the grave slabs. In the first, a leather belt is wrapped around the waist, its strap ends thread through the bronze ring then fold back along the inside of the belt to be held in place by two bronze studs (studs that are either punched through the two thicknesses of belt leather, or that are a built onto the ring). A second style, equally popular,

Damianus, a *beneficarius* from Alexandria in Egypt (*after Simon James*)

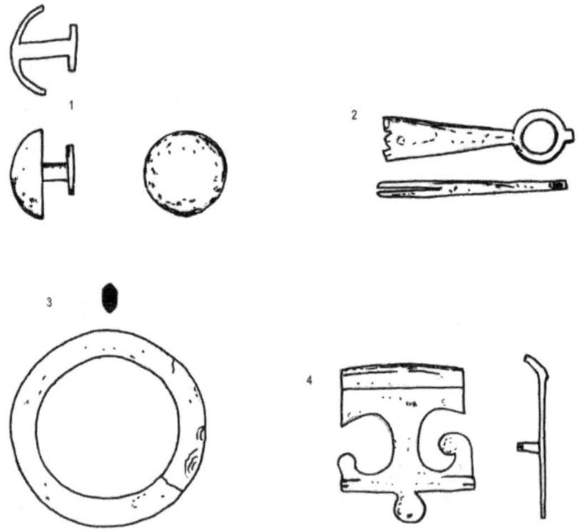

Belt fittings from Lauriacum (modern Enns). 1 mushroom-shaped stud; 2 belt strap-end; 3 ring buckle; 4 decorative belt plate. (*after Hans-Jörg Ubl*)

has the strap ends of the belt still held in place with bronze studs, but the end that fed through the right-hand side is much longer (somewhere between 50–80 cm), hanging below the belt as a curved 'swag', it is tucked up under the belt and a loop of the strap sticks up above the belt. The rest of the belt end tucks behind the belt and is allowed to trail onto the soldier's right thigh. When a belt is shown with a long tail in this way, it is nearly always depicted as split into two near the end with a bronze pendant decorating the very end of each belt strap. It is these dangling metal fittings that Daminaus and others are shown fidgeting with. A reconstruction of this belt confirms that the strap ends clash and jangle together while walking, recreating that noisy, attention grabbing effect created by the studded aprons of earlier legionaries.

High quality carvings, such as a horseman of the imperial horse guard (*equites singulares*)[8] and a military horn-player on the Ludovisi Battle Sarcophagus, show that some (or all) belts were decorated with stitched borders. The Terentius fresco provides further details, it depicts soldiers of low rank alongside their commanding officer. Of significance is the fact that tribune Terentius' belt is red, while those of his men are brown, representing un-dyed leather. Was the tribune's belt dyed or painted? Certainly it tells us that although soldiers, officers and even emperors seemed to be wearing the same style of military clothing, visible distinctions of rank and status did exist.

Some belt fittings from this period suggest that loops and attachment points were fitted to belts in order that small items of kit (purses or knives, for example) might be hung from them. One would expect that a dagger would also hang from this belt, as it had done from the military belts of soldiers fighting for Trajan a century earlier. However, none of the tomb-stone veterans are shown wearing daggers in this way, or, to be frank, wearing daggers at all – yet we still find them on military sites. Perhaps daggers were worn from baldrics, slung over the shoulder. The author experimented with a dagger suspension system, adding a third bronze stud and hanging the dagger from two of them.

Swords are shown within scabbards that hang from a wide shoulder strap (a baldric). This was an innovation – not only did it allow the sword to hang on the soldier's left-hand side but it fastened in a new and unusual way. The baldric was broad (probably for show) and featured a decorative bronze disc (*phalera*) that pierced the leather with a small metal loop protruding from its back. To enable the leather baldric to fasten around the scabbard it narrowed to a thin thread and was tied around the scabbard and through a metal or bone scabbard slide. This slide was also an innovation, a fitting on the front of the sword scabbard pierced with a slot that the narrow baldric thread could feed through. Once fed through the slide securely the narrow strap end of the baldric then returned to the back of the wide baldric and was tied onto the *phalera's* metal loop, out of sight. Two baldrics from Vimose in Denmark give us actual dimensions (width 80 mm and 86 mm) and evidence of decorative stitching, in one case featuring a dolphin on the broad end of the strap, just below the *phalera*.

Phalera were conspicuously placed. Although many found on the German frontier are in the form of plain bronze discs, those from other sites boast elaborate openwork decoration or display Celtic designs, spokes or swastika motifs. A number of examples of an openwork eagle clutching the thunderbolts

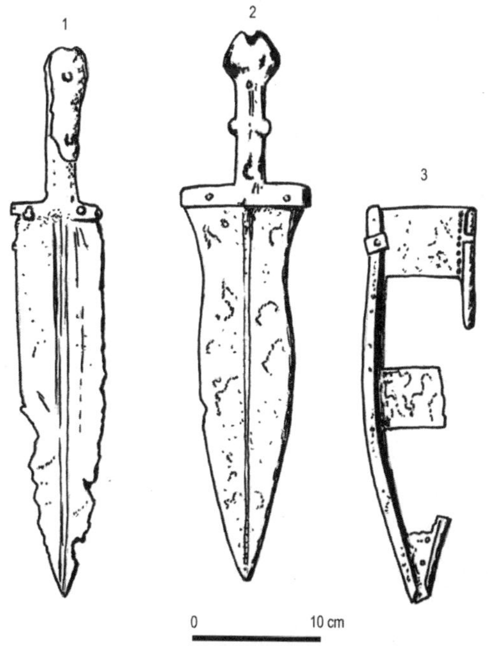

Third century daggers from the Künzing hoard. (*after Bishop and Coulston*)

of Jupiter have been found, complete with the words '*OPTIME MAXIME CON(serva)*', picked out around the disc. Examples of this *phalera* come from Lauriacum, Carlisle, Strasbourg and other forts both in Britain and Germany.

Where did such an ingenious attachment method come from? It did not resemble any previous Roman suspension system. Similarly, how did the men of the legions come to adopt the strange 'buckle-less' ring belt? Presumably we must look to the northern tribes, source of inspiration for the new legionary clothing fashions .... and yet there is no hint of any ring belt or wide sword baldric amongst the German tribes. Instead our focus must be on Rome's other major frontier, and to its eastern rival, Sassanid Persia. Here, warriors displaying ring buckle belts, complete with strap ends hanging in distinctive swags just like Roman belts, appear on sculpted reliefs at Bishapur. Other (pre-Sassanian) depictions exist from Palmyra and northern Mesopotamia featuring belts with hanging strap ends. These predate the third century, suggesting that the legions adopted the fashion from the east. Archaeology also supports this theory: ring buckles with studs have no forerunners within the Roman Empire, but do have parallels within Iran and Luristan.

Did the wide baldric also originate in the east? In fact, there are depictions from Bishapur and Carrhae of warriors wearing almost identical sword belts, but, unlike the men of the legions these belts were worn around the waist. Yet they feature the wide decorative end tapering to a narrow strap end that threads through a scabbard slide. Just like the Roman baldric this strap end then fastens behind a circular metal plate. This left the sword hanging low from the waist, perfectly acceptable for an eastern horse-riding aristocrat. However, the Roman infantrymen needed the sword out of the way of his legs and so, worn over the shoulder the pommel of the Roman sword (the *spatha*) was raised up to armpit height. Roman cavalrymen also utilised this over-the shoulder-sword belt, no doubt due to the homogenization of Roman military equipment.

The Rome-Parthian frontier was no Berlin Wall. Legionaries did not stare uneasily across the stony desert at rich Parthian caravan cities, whose garrisons gazed impassively back. Syria and northern Mesopotamia was a cultural melting pot, a frontier 'zone' that at some periods was Roman, at others Parthian, and that was home to Arabs, Greeks, Jews, Syrians, Assyrians, Romans and Parthians on a more-or-less permanent basis. Legions based here were exposed to a huge amount of cultural influence. Not only that but during the two massive invasions of Parthia during the reigns of Marcus Aurelius (165) and Septimius Severus (197) the legions were deep within enemy territory. Eastern legions must have been the first to adopt the Parthian belt and baldric styles, both from their experiences on the battlefield and from the recruitment of local people who favoured such fashions.[9]

Exactly 'when' the ring buckles and wide baldrics were adopted is unknown. Had some event triggered the new fashion? The cultural influences of the region had of course been in effect ever since the Romans arrived two centuries ago, so what had changed? It may be that, just as the Danubian troops were slowly switching to a northern European clothing style following the decades after the Marcomannic Wars, the eastern legions were likewise embracing the Parthian belt buckle at a leisurely decade-by-decade pace. Yet, the new fashion exploded across the empire suddenly after appearing on the tombstones of the II Parthica veterans at Apamea. That dates the earliest representation of the fashion to 216, the year of Emperor Caracalla's Persian campaign. Perhaps soldiers wore the belts prior to this until it suddenly became 'cool' to be seen on one's official statuary with them. Perhaps the wearing of the ring buckle actually dates from

Eastern nobles wearing sword-belts and ring-buckles. (*after Simon James*)

the reign of Caracalla, or more likely from the period of Septimius Severus' grand eastern invasion. Adopted by his expeditionary armies (on campaign in hostile Mesopotamia in 195, 197 and 198), enough time would have passed for the fashion to become *de rigeur* by Caracalla's day.

The Cloak

Cloaks might seem from the perspective of the 21st century to be an item of outdoor wear, something to ward off rain or chill evening air. Yet they were also an item of fashion, soldiers garrisoned in the baking Syrian sun still donned cloaks. The troops of the general Saturninus wore heavy cloaks in winter and light ones during the summer.[10] A large rectangular cloak known as a *sagum* (or *sagum militaria*) is often depicted on eastern tombstones, and the men of Terentius' cohort at Dura Europus are shown at the altar, worshipping in their military cloaks.

The *sagum* had a long history, it was a thick, military cloak of Gallic origin that was itself a symbol of war. For the Roman soldier this essential piece of kit served as a blanket, a wet-weather poncho and a First World War trench-coat. It is likely that the wool's natural oil (lanolin) was retained to provide a good measure of water-proofing. Lanolin would be lost during any dyeing process which may explain why the military cloak is often a standard colour. While civilians wore fashionably coloured cloaks of various styles, the legions left theirs un-dyed. In frescoes the cloak appears yellow-brown or chocolate brown, the natural colour of the sheep from which the wool taken.

Officers like tribune Terentius were an exception, they preferred to wear white cloaks. White served as a mark of status since it was difficult to keep clean and would have required regular laundering. A small number of cloaks have been illustrated as red, perhaps suggesting that the wearer is another type of officer, perhaps a centurion.[11]

The wall-painting on which Terentius and his men appear crisply details the cloaks they wear, not just the colour but also the way in which they are folded and draped. Just like the cloaks on many third century tomb reliefs, the Terentius cloaks are fastened on the right shoulder with a metal brooch. Wearing a cloak this way gives the right arm freedom to move, and it allows the cloak to fall along the left side of the body, often covering the left arm. When some activity is required, or the cloak simply needs to be pushed out of the way (for example at the Dura temple service), the hanging portion can be lifted and flicked back over the left shoulder. One might imagine that a cloak would be discarded in combat, yet at Dura Europus where the remnants of battle litter siege tunnels beneath the city walls, several Roman brooches were found, the cloaks having crumbled away long ago. Not only had this been a fierce hand-to-hand scrap, but it was one that had been fought within a confined and restricted space. Were the Roman troops *that* attached to their cloaks?

Few cloaks from this period have survived and where they do they might easily have been mis-identified as a blanket. In fact, the papyrus document BGU VII 1564 includes an order for several cloaks and they are identical in size to a blanket on the same list. Only the tell-tale cloak brooch, pinned to the fabric, is a guarantee that archaeologists are dealing with a cloak. The rich Thorsberg assemblage, yielding swords, spears, clothing and other artefacts may have included a cloak. It features a tablet-woven border and measures 1.68 m by 2.50 m.[12] Military *saga,* like those on the Egyptian papyrus, seem to have been woven to a similar size; the four cloaks on that list are 2.66 m long by 1.77 m, while a cloak discovered at Nahal Hever in the Judean desert is 2.7 m by 1.4 m. A smaller cloak found in Nubia is only 1.75 m long and 1.05 m wide.

Brooches found in military contexts were typically of bronze but could be silver or gold, indeed some of the most eye-catching are valuable gem-encrusted examples. As with belt buckles, fashions changed with the wind and this fact often allows archaeologists to date them to a certain century. Styles were transmitted quickly across the empire and a typical assemblage of cloak brooches on the Rhine in the third century might easily resemble one on the Danube or along Hadrian's Wall. The most common types are the 'plate' brooch (which resembles a modern pin-badge – a patterned plate with a locking pin at the back) and the 'bow brooch'. The best analogy for this latter type of brooch is that of a giant safety pin! A new style of bow brooch, the cross-bow, makes its debut in the third century; it is named after its similarity to the medieval weapon. During the fourth century, the crossbow brooch would dominate military fashion, becoming almost a mark of government authority.

In Emperor Trajan's day a hooded cape (*paenula*) had also been popular, but this item disappears from representations from the late second century onward. It may be that the impact of Severus may also be felt here, author Graham Sumner has suggested that the hooded *paenula* might have been particularly associated with the Praetorian Guard. Once this body was discredited and disbanded, its signature cloak may have fallen out of favour.[13]

Civilians in the third century preferred to wear capes when outdoors. Soldiers found capes especially useful in places like Germany and Britain, where the weather could turn nasty and the winters were bitterly cold. Local Germans in the late second century had been wearing ankle-length capes for years and it seems the legionaries liked and used them too. They called this cloak the *caracallus*. Through the intervention of Severus' son, Caracalla, hooded capes once again become popular in the third century. This emperor gained his nickname from the way he wore the local German cloak when on campaign on the Rhine in 213. While he was dressing as a soldier in order to court the loyalty of the legions, they, in turn were copying him. The emperor and his wife served as an essential 'fashion-plate' for new trends throughout the empire. The *caracallus* caught on. In Britain the long hooded cape was instead called the *cucullus*, and nicknamed the *'birrus Britannicus'*.

Popular with farmers, travellers and others spending time outdoors, the *alicula* was a short cape with a hood that covered the shoulders. Most representations show that it was stitched up at the front. Many sculptures show the *alicula* with a 'stippled' texture almost as if it were made of thick wool or fleece. At least one representation (a small statue of a Roman ploughman found at Triers in France) shows a farm-worker in a goatskin *alicula*. Easy to pack, and useful in bad weather, the *alicula* may have been popular with soldiers on the march. One stone relief from Cordoba, in Spain, does show the shoulders and torso of a soldier wearing ringmail. He also wears a textured *alicula*, fastened together, not by stitching, but instead by a clasp of some sort. The figure seems to be in a line with two other individuals, also wearing these shoulder capes, though it is not known whether these men are also soldiers.

A 'Danubian Fashion'?

Fashion has rarely been about individuals seeing new clothing designs they like and then adopting them. Fashion change is about belonging, about making a conscious decision to associate with a group, a movement or cultural meme through an overt display.

Settled on the edge of barbarian territory, the legions of the Danube frontier had been recruiting locals into their ranks since the Marcomannic Wars. Many of these Moesians and Pannonians wore long-sleeved tunics and trousers. Similarly, subjugated tribes were often forced by treaty to supply the Roman auxiliaries with *dalmatic*-wearing recruits. It could be that the Danubian garrisons began this trend, stuck in the Marcomannic war-zone and rarely sending out *vexillations* to other frontiers. The peculiar barbarian fashions may have had little chance to be diluted by the Roman 'norm'. It might have been a trend that began in the 160s and developed over a decade or two, until the emperor Septimius Severus marched these combat-hardened legions into Rome in 193. Dio Cassius reported how shocked the people of Rome were to see a 'throng of motley soldiers most savage in appearance' behaving badly within the city's boundaries.

Had the Danube legions brought with them into the capital the barbaric frontier costume of the Pannonians, Moesians and Germans? If they had, then how did this new fashion for trousers and long-sleeved tunics soon gain currency amongst all of the other legions scattered across the empire? By the mid-third century, as we have seen, the combination proved so popular that all soldiers of all ranks had adopted it. At this one time in Roman history, it would not be amiss to talk almost of a legionary 'uniform'.

Perhaps the answer might be found in the events of 193. When Severus took control of the capital he immediately disbanded the (mostly Italian-born) Praetorian Guard and replaced them with picked troops from his loyal Danubian regiments. In that same year he conducted a levy (*dilectus*) within Italy, which historian Ross Cowan believes may have marked the formation of Legio II Parthica. This first Italian batch of recruits cannot have come close to filling the new cohorts and so, as he marched eastward toward his confrontation with Pescennius Niger, he added to it Thracian recruits. Almost certainly the officers, centurions and drill-masters would be made up of experienced men plucked from his Danubian veterans. This was an established practice. Large numbers of legionaries and auxiliaries from the Moesian garrisons were already in Thrace besieging the hostile city of Byzantium. These men under Marius Maximus were an obvious source of experienced troops for Severus' new legion. Fabius Clio, another lieutenant of Severus, was also operating in the region, and with his Danubian troops had just prevented Niger from capturing the city of Perinthus. Rewards of transfer to an elite unit such as Legio II or the Guard were common for such bravery amongst the ranks.

Evidence of direct transfers from the Danubian units into Legio II eludes us, but one military anomaly does seem to add weight to the idea. The 80-man century, the crucial building block of any legion, was normally named after its commander, its centurion. When Roman troops operated in *vexillations*, different centuries and cohorts from different legions working together, that practice was dropped in favour of naming a century after its tactical role in the combat formation; for example, VII *princeps prior* (the *princeps prior* century of the seventh cohort). Michael Speidel suggested that II Parthica was raised in the main from established legionary detachments because it used this distinctive *vexillation* naming system even though it was an established legion.

The two elite units of the Roman Empire, the Praetorian Guard and Legio II Parthica, were most probably filled with these Danubian veterans. Legio II was the last legion to ever deploy in its entirety to a combat zone (in 197). After this it joined the practice of the Guard and the rest of the legions in dispatching *vexillations* to hot-spots or to add man-power to an expedition. Any barbarian fashions picked up on the banks of the Danube would be quickly disseminated across the empire from garrison to garrison as troops came into contact with Praetorians or the II Parthicans. The cachet that they and their officers enjoyed as the emperor's crack troops would certainly have inspired imitation amongst the regular units. Criss-crossing the empire, meeting troops from far distant locations who had also been dispatched within a *vexillation*, the Danubian troops could have carried their fashion sense with them. We know that throughout history peoples of lower status have always looked upwards to those of high status in order to replicate the fashions on display. Women throughout Rome peered at the new coin issues to imitate each new hair-style of the empress. Soldiers did likewise, growing full beards during the reign of Emperor Hadrian, cutting their hair short and wearing a close-cropped beard during the early third century, and going clean shaven under the reign of beard-less Constantine.

5

Sword And Shield

'A number [of corpses] had fallen by sling-shot or had been transfixed by shafts tipped with metal. In some cases the head had been split in two by a sword-stroke through crown and forehead, and hung down on both shoulders, a most gruesome sight.'

Ammianus Marcellinus 31.7

Few of the famous warriors of history are so closely associated with their weaponry as are the Roman legionaries with their *gladius*. Yes, the Ghurkas have their curved kukri knives, the samurai had their legendary *katana* and the Vikings were renowned for their use of the battle axe, but no army has done so much on the point of a single weapon as did the Roman *milites*. Yet, in the mid-second century, the legions swapped the famous *gladius* for the much longer *spatha*. This chapter looks at both weapons and explores the possible reasons for the change as well as the swords' relationship with the shields of the day.

The Gladius

Like most Roman military equipment, the famous Roman shortsword was first encountered in the hands of a rival nation and, once it been defeated, the sword was swiftly adopted. The legions had fought the Carthaginians in Spain as commercial rivalries during the third century BC, four hundred years before the reign of Septimius Severus. The armies of Carthage were composed in the main of mercenary forces and the Iberian tribes of Spain were skilled mercenary fighters. During the first two Punic Wars the Romans encountered and began to adopt the 'Spanish sword' that was being used with great effect by these Iberians. It was a weapon that the Romans would call the *gladius Hispaniensis*.

From around 200 BC the *gladius*, a shortsword just over 60 cm long with a wickedly sharp tip and a sinuous, waisted blade became the Roman sidearm of choice. The legions adopted not just the deadly blade, however, but also the Iberian scabbard with its ring suspension system and its accompanying dagger, the *pugio*. Although the sword was almost certainly taken up on its own bloody merits, the more utilitarian sword and dagger scabbards seem to have been retained in order to display their Hispanic derivations. They changed little during the next three centuries. In fact, one can see a 'martial tradition' at play through the continued wearing of these Spanish scabbards. Each one had four rings, two on either side, which were intended for attachment to a military belt. Roman soldiers only ever used the top two rings in order to tie their sword and dagger scabbards to their belts ... the lower rings were almost always left to hang useless and unused. These Spanish-derived scabbards were a fashion, a regimental trophy that harkened back to the Punic Wars, the most bitter and momentous conflicts of Rome's history.

The *gladius* developed and evolved during those three hundred years. During the reign of the first emperor, Augustus, the new 'Mainz' pattern was shorter (around 50 cm) and slowly began to get broader and broader. While the 'waist' of the blade was not as pronounced, the tip became extremely long and pointed. Variants existed, such as the 'Nauportus' and the 'Fontillet' types, but the Mainz predominated until the mid-first century AD. From then on a new design became popular with the legions; it was named by archaeologists the 'Pompeii' type *gladius* after a number of examples were uncovered in that buried city. More recently, in 1981, a Pompeii *gladius* was discovered with the body of a Roman soldier found at Herculaneum. The Pompeii type featured a short, triangular point and its blade edges were parallel, rather than tapering or waisted.

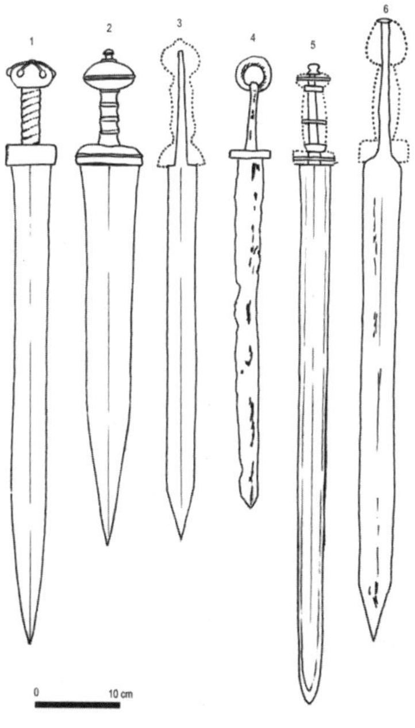

Roman swords. 1 Republican *gladius Hispaniensis*; 2 early imperial Mainz gladius; 3 early imperial Pompeii gladius; 4 Antonine ring-pommel sword; 5 Straubing-Nydam style *spatha*; 6 Lauriacum-Hromowka style *spatha*. (*after Simon James*)

Did the sword allow Roman troops to fight in new, more aggressive ways? In fact the reverse may equally have been true with the *gladius Hispaniensis* being adopted because it perfectly suited the Roman way of war. The famous Roman tactic of thrusting low into the opponent's body with the sword may have predated the adoption of this new weapon. Written accounts of the sword in use illustrate its particular strengths. During a battle against the Gauls in 360 BC, Titus Manlius 'Torquatus' fought a duel with a Gallic hero:

> The ...Gaul held out his shield ... to meet his adversary's blows and aimed a tremendous cut downwards with his sword. [Manlius] evaded the blow and, pushing aside the bottom of the Gaul's shield with his own, he slipped under it close up to the Gaul, too near for him to get at him with his sword. Then, turning the point of his blade upwards, he gave two rapid thrusts in succession and stabbed the Gaul in the belly and the groin, laying his enemy prostrate ...
>
> Livy 7.10

An account written by Dionysus of Halicarnassus describes how the legionaries

> would duck under [the arms of the Gauls], holding up their shields, and then stooping and crouching low ... they would strike their opponents in the groins, pierce their sides and drive their blows through their breasts into their vitals.
>
> Dionysus of Halicarnassus 14.10

Both Dionysus and Livy wrote in the first century BC, well after the events they were describing and they were recounting fighting techniques of their own time. Nonetheless, their vivid battle descriptions paint a clear image of how these swords were supposed to be employed. The *gladius* suited this type of close-in combat and perfectly complemented the large, curved body shield carried by the troops of the day. As the *gladius* developed in the ensuing centuries, a preference for shorter blade lengths slowly emerged. Such reductions only emphasise the increasingly aggressive nature of Roman combat training with the imperative to get in close. A relief from the fort headquarters building at Mainz depicts a legionary in such a stance. Left leg forward, crouching low with a shield held up to his face, his *gladius* is in his right hand just below waist height ready to thrust forward into an opponent's belly.

Other fighting moves were possible; it is clear that Roman soldiers did use their shortswords to chop, hack and slice at their opponents. Once Trajan had defeated the Dacians at the Battle of Tapae in AD 102, his troops constructed a monument to commemorate the victory. This monument, called the Tropaeum Traiani, at Adamclissi, is decorated with a series of combat reliefs that illustrate several Roman attack postures. There is the classic stab into the belly with shield held high, another depicts a legionary readying his blade to swing it overarm down onto a kneeling Dacian. Yet another shows a Roman soldier with his

Legionaries of emperor Vespasian in combat, from Mainz. (*after Graham Sumner*)

gladius reversed, point down, stabbing into the neck of a falling warrior. Unlike the scenes depicted on Trajan's Column in Rome, these savage but realistic combat recreations were carved by the soldiers themselves; we can be sure that these reliefs reflect a terrible battlefield reality.

The Dacian Wars lasted until 106, but Trajan did not stop there. He marched on Armenia and northern Mesopotamia and was the first Roman emperor ever to sack Ctesiphon, the formidable capital of the Parthian kingdom. His soldiers fought with the Pompeii-style *gladius*, they fought and conquered in his name.

The Rectangular Scutum

The Roman fighting style, the get-in-close approach, could only work with the protection of a large body shield (*scutum*). This shield took a variety of forms in the first century AD, while some were flat the most famous and probably most commonly used shield design was curved and rectangular. This is the defining symbol of the Roman soldier in movies, books and TV.

Trajan's Column and the Tropaeum Traiani show legionaries using the curved rectangular shield in hand-to-hand fighting. It was almost certainly a native invention, and although evolving in form over the centuries, it continued to be depicted in use by legionaries alone. Auxiliary soldiers instead are seen using flat shields, often oval in shape. This differentiation held true throughout the first two centuries of the Roman Empire.

Parts of metallic shield edging as well as bosses and leather covers have been found from across the empire but only one intact shield from the imperial period has so far been recovered. This *scutum* from Dura Europus is dated to the mid-third century but appears to be the same shield used by legionaries of early periods, including those on Trajan's Column. It is rectangular in shape, 102 cm in height and 83 cm wide (and measuring 66 cm across the curve from edge to edge). It has a plywood construction which enabled the shield-makers to create that famous curve. Strips of wood between 30 mm and 50 mm wide were glued together in three superimposed layers to provide strength and rigidity. A circular hole was cut in the centre and a wooden bar crossed this opening to act as a hand-hold. Other bars, some running top to bottom, others running across the width of the shield, were pegged and glued onto the back as a method of reinforcement. *See* Colour Plate 14.

While the edge of this particular example was protected by a strip of stitched-on rawhide, it is clear that earlier shields of this type were edged with bronze, nailed securely in place. This prevented the wood splitting when chopped by an opponent's blade. Similarly, although no boss (*umbo*) was found with the shield, many examples have been recovered from earlier military sites and all Roman shields are depicted with them in place. These iron or bronze hemispherical items were riveted over the circular hole in the shield board and protected the hand from enemy blows. Members of auxiliary cohorts fighting at Mons Graupius in AD 83 also used their shield bosses offensively, punching at their Caledonian enemies.[1]

Unlike the shields carried by medieval knights or Greek hoplites, the Roman *scutum* was held by its owner in a horizontal grip, without leather straps to support the weight. These shields were heavy; without the missing boss the Dura example weighed around 5.5 kg. Estimates do vary, but earlier shields like those depicted on Trajan's Column may have weighed as much as 7.5 kg. Peter Connolly believed that the Dura shield may be on the light side and that earlier examples were probably thicker, forcing an increase in weight. The boss and metallic edging all contribute to the 7.5 kg total.[2]

Auxiliary troops were instead issued with a flat shield, often oval in shape. Oval designs are represented on the Tropeum Traiani as well as the Mainz column base and Trajan's Column. Leather shield covers outlining an oval shield board have also been found. Yet there were other designs of flat shield in use by *auxilia*, both rectangular and hexagonal and these were most likely formed of thin layers of plywood and then edged with bronze. Like the curved *scutum* of the legionaries they were reinforced with wooden batons on the reverse, edged with metal fitted with a bronze or iron boss on the front.

Why did the legionaries and the auxiliaries fight with very different kinds of shields? As we have seen, the *gladius* sword perfectly suited the close-in, short-range fighting style of the Roman legionary. *Gladius* and curved *scutum* made a lethal combination. The auxiliaries were also equipped with this sword but their primary weapon was actually the spear, not the sword. It seems that spear-fighting required a flat (rather than a curved) shield to be in any way effective. It allowed more freedom of movement and it could be used in partnership with the spear, the javelin and of course, the *gladius*. After all, the strength of the *auxilia* was versatility.[3]

All-Change: The Antonine Revolution

Historians generally agree that Emperor Hadrian, at the end of the first quarter of the second century, halted the expansion of the Roman empire. He is remembered as a consolidator, touring his empire and strengthening frontiers in Germany and Britain. In the century that had just passed, more Roman territory had been gained through bloody conquest than at any other period in Roman history. Egypt, Mauretania, Britain, the Danubian provinces, Spain, Dacia, Arabia, Cappadocia and Galatia in central Turkey were all acquired from the reign of Emperor Augustus onwards. Practically all of these new territories were gained by force, and if the pairing of curved rectangular *scutum* and *gladius* could bring these kinds of victories, why would anyone give them up?

Yet change to the military hardware of the legions *did* occur, and it probably began shortly after the death of Hadrian. His adopted son and heir, Antoninus Pius, reigned for twenty-three years, from July 138 to March 161. There is no reason to suppose that this emperor had change in mind, that he actively promoted the use of new military kit or that he ordered the legionary commanders to adopt new patterns of swords and shields. The Roman military system just did not work like that. With its structure, regimentation and logistical expertise, it is often easy to compare the Roman army favourably with its modern military equivalent. In our world, when a new weapon or helmet is developed it is sent out to the troops in their garrisons for immediate adoption. There may be a time lag in getting the new piece of kit to all the units, but eventually everyone has the new M16A2, the Osprey Mk 4 Body Armour, the M1967 Individual Load Carrying Equipment gear, or whatever.

Communication, transportation and manufacturing differences exist between armies of today and the legions of Rome. Imperial Rome had a radically different approach to the acquisition of weaponry than today's reliance on civilian defence contractors. In areas of urbanisation, such as the wealthy cities of the east, arms and armour were manufactured in civilian workshops (*fabricae*). On the northern borders the armies were far from long-established urban areas and probably manned the *fabricae* themselves. They were located either inside their fortresses or within the adjacent settlements (*vici*).[4]

It is likely that innovations in weaponry and armour spread from one legion to another via the transfer of individual soldiers, *vexillations* and officers (most notably the centurions, those keepers of military knowledge and tradition). A centurion who accepted promotion from a legion in Dacia, to one in Wales (for example) might recommend some new innovation or style of sword to his new unit. He might be wearing a new helmet type or carry a modification of the typical *gladius* that both his colleagues and his own subordinates would seek to emulate. 'Instances of ... mutual emulation,' says Simon James, 'are then to be expected (through swapping, purchase, theft, looting or copying) [helping] to erode any ... regional distinctions between provincial armies.'[5]

Short swords continue to be depicted in Roman art through the middle of the second century. While the troops did continue to use the Pompeii *gladius* through this period, some were sheathing a new type of short sword: the *Ringknaufschwerter* or 'ring-pommel' sword. An example dated to the mid-second century comes from Wehringen, near Augsburg in Germany, another was found at Geneva but was later in date (around AD 180). These are early examples; the ring-pommel sword, so-called because its grip terminates in a prominent iron ring, became much more common at the end of the second century and its popularity increased during the third. These weapons featured a tapering blade and a tang (ending in the eponymous ring) which served as the handgrip. In length the blades themselves ranged from around 35 cm (the Steinamenger sword) up to around 48 cm (the Hamfelde and Linz swords). Of a comparable size and weight to the Pompeii *gladius*, the ring-pommel sword seems to have been a fashionable alternative to the older design, an alternative that was becoming popular with troops in northern Gaul, the Rhine frontier and the upper Danube. The design was not of course Roman in origin; the *Ringknaufschwerter* first appear on Sarmatian gravestones from the first century AD. Examples that must have served as the inspiration for Roman adoption have been found amongst the German tribes that dwelt beyond the northern frontier. One cannot help but tie the mid-second century introduction of this new Sarmatian-style sword to the Marcomannic Wars which forced Romans and Sarmatians together for over a dozen years.

> Given time, the fighting itself will cause the two sides to become more like each other, even to the point where opposites converge, merge and change places ... The principle reason behind this phenomenon is that war represents perhaps the most imitative activity known to man.
>
> Van Crefeld, *Transformation of War, 1991, p. 174*

Almost certainly, an innovative new method of suspending the sword was imported along with the *Ringknaufschwerter*. We saw this happen with the *gladius Hispaniensis* following the Punic Wars. Iberian-style ring-suspension came hand-in-hand with the Iberian scabbard and sword as a fashionable military package. Swords in the late second century now began to be suspended from a metal bracket (a 'slide') attached to the front face of the scabbard. The soldier's baldric or shoulder-belt passed behind this slide. One of these sword slides first appears on the tombstone of a soldier found at Aquincum (modern Budapest), tentatively dated to either the reign of Hadrian or Antoninus Pius. Before that, these distinctive scabbard slides had only appeared on Trajan's Column, worn in battle by 'barbarian' troops. By the end of the second century all Roman swords were being suspended in this way.[6]

In the third century, slides would follow their own fashions, often they were made of copper alloy or iron, while others were carved from bone or even ivory. Elaborate dolphin-shaped slides are known and one fine example comes from South Shields in northern England. The tip of a Roman scabbard was always protected by a metallic 'chape'; in the late second century these evolved into a number of specific styles. Prominent on gravestones were the disc-shaped chapes, often elaborately decorated; other types included rectangular 'box' chapes and peltate (or crescent) chapes. The sword grips themselves were caught up with the change in fashion; plain, ribbed and fluted types were common and they were made either of bone or wood. They differed markedly from the knobbly grips often found on earlier shortswords.

Triumph of the Long Sword

While Roman infantry were marching into battle with the *gladius* or the more fashionable *Ringknaufschwerter*, Roman cavalry were sticking with their longer cavalry sword, the *spatha*. With its longer reach and added weight intended for slashing attacks, the *spatha* was far handier in mounted combat than a short stabbing blade. Soon the infantry would be carrying this weapon as well.

Changes in the type of sword favoured by the legions continued throughout the second century and by AD 200 a longer cavalry-type *spatha* had been adopted almost universally by the Roman foot soldiers, suspended from a baldric on a Sarmatian-style scabbard slide (of course). It was the long *spatha* which would dominate the Roman armoury from that date through to the end of the Roman Empire and there was never any real return to the short stabbing sword. Since the *gladius* told us much about the fighting style of the legionary, this change in primary weapon also tells us that the way in which the Roman *milites* fought changed too.

A key piece of evidence in this chronological jigsaw comes from Lyons, in southern France. Here a Roman soldier was found in a hasty burial in the Rue des Fantasques, close to the Bridge of Lattre de Tassigny over the River Rhône. The soldier's purse contained twelve silver denarii and the latest of these was dated to 194, the fledgling reign of Septimius Severus. It is generally accepted that this soldier was a casualty of Severus' great battle against the forces of Clodius Albinus that took place outside Roman Lyon (Lugdunum) in 197.[7]

A *spatha* with a broken tip was found with the soldier, its scabbard had been fitted with a heart-shaped chape and a palm-leaf scabbard slide. The wide baldric, the earliest one found, and the decorative disc (*phalera*) that became such a feature of Roman military kit in the third century had been worn by the man during the battle. Although the leather had rotted away, the concentric *phalera* and the open-work metal terminal that hung from the end of the baldric, remained. Here is the evidence that the legions had adopted the *spatha* along with the Sarmatian scabbard slide and wide Parthian-style baldric.

Since swords were rarely buried with soldiers, the bulk of the *spatha* finds from the third century come from ritual deposits in barbarian Germany with great levels of preservation. Swords, baldrics and scabbards were found in excellent condition at Nydam, Illerup and Vimose, in Denmark, and at Thorsberg in Germany, close to the Danish border. The blades are often beautifully pattern-welded, a technique of sword-making that used several iron bars with differing carbon contents to form a core that was twisted and then folded and hammered repeatedly. The result was a strong and flexible core of a sword to which hard cutting edges could then be welded.

Two main types of *spatha* have been identified, the long, narrow 'Straubing-Nydam' type and the shorter and wider 'Lauriacum-Hromowka' type. The longer Straubing blades have a length between 65 and 80 cm (and a maximum width of 4.4 cm) while the shorter Lauriacum type of blade varies in length from 55 to 65 cm (with a width between 6 and 7.5 cm). Remember that examples of the *gladius*, during the first century AD, could reach 50 to 55 cm in length. Although we call the *spatha* a 'long' sword it should really be classified as a 'medium' sword. None of the examples reach the prodigious lengths (in excess of 100 cm) of medieval blades: the *langes Schwert*, Scottish claymore, German *Zweihänder* and others.

Swords belonging to the Lauriacum type are wide with parallel edges and their blades end in a triangular point similar in form to that of the Pompeii *gladius*. Appearing around the mid-second century and continuing into the third, they may have evolved directly from the Pompeii *gladius*. Straubing blades are generally longer and taper to a point, they appear in the late second century, continuing through into the fourth. This slightly later form of the *spatha* may be derived from the tapering, arch-pointed, ring-pommel sword. The trend in Roman arms was for longer swords, a reversal of the shortening of the *gladius*

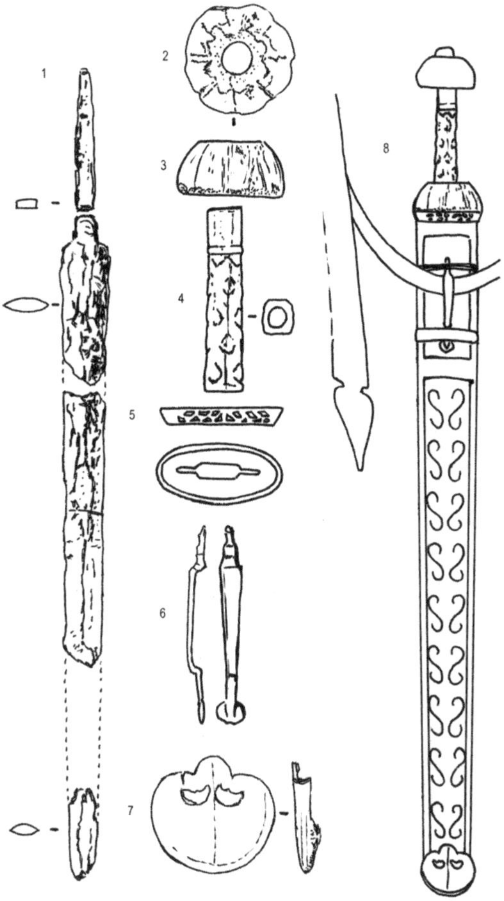

Sword components from Dura Europus. 1 blade; 2,3 rock crystal pommel; 4 bone grip; 5 hilt guard; 6 scabbard slide; 7 scabbard chape; 8 reconstructed sword. (*after Simon James*)

at the beginning of the imperial period. In the early second century most blades are around 50 cm long, with a minority reaching 60 or 70 cm. In the latter half of the second century around 50 per cent of blades were now over 60 cm in length with a minority reaching 70 cm.[8]

It could be that the new pattern-welding techniques introduced from Germany produced stronger blades and enabled the fashioning of longer swords. Yet this does not explain why Roman troops were demanding a longer weapon in the first place. The war-winning Roman combat technique of ducking low and thrusting up into an opponent's groin and belly had relied on the short *gladius*. Was the move to a longer sword a move away from this fighting style? If it was, why?

Other changes were occurring simultaneously, in both helmet and shield design. The rectangular, curved shield had perfectly complemented the offensive capability of the thrusting *gladius*; likewise, the new-style third century shield 'must' have been linked inextricably with the way in which the *spatha* was being used.

A New, Oval Shield

In the Imperial Forum of Rome stands the triumphal Arch of Septimius Severus. Completed around 204, it marked his successful sacking of Ctesiphon and victory over the Parthians. It would be folly to study the battle scenes on the arch looking for accurate representations of third century equipment, nevertheless there is some merit in investigating just how the sculptors depicted Severus' legionaries. While details may be wrong and some classical tropes re-used, one aspect of the military equipment immediately strikes the observer: where are all the curved cylindrical shields that littered the Columns of Trajan and Marcus Aurelius? Soldiers on the arch carry a large, broad oval shield. Many of these soldiers wear *lorica segmentata*, which is a form of armour that archaeologists associate only with the legionary. A purely artistic rendering would surely have them all equipped with the rectangular *scutum*.

Of course we have hindsight; throughout the third century, wall-paintings, tombstones and sculpture all depict the new oval design of shield. The curved legionary shield is rarely seen, although a famous example was uncovered at the Syrian fortress of Dura Europus along with a cache of large, oval types. By AD 200 then, and probably at least a decade or two before, the legions of Rome had swapped their classic rectangular shield for an oval replacement.[9]

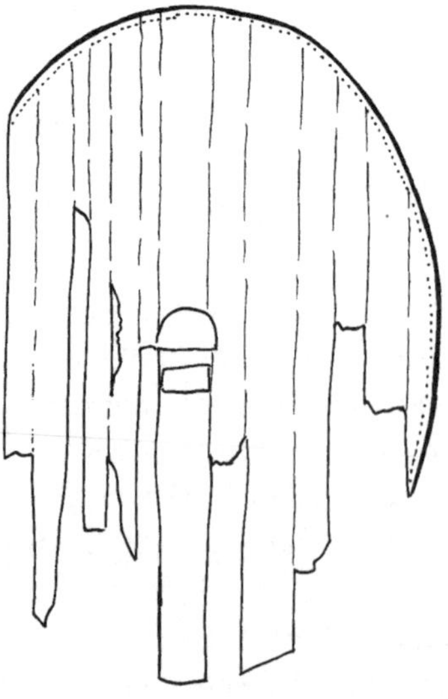

Shield V from Dura Europus. (*after Rostovtzeff*)

From Dura, twenty-four complete or fragmentary oval shields were found, providing us with a wonderful insight into this new defensive technology. Unlike the curved shields, these were constructed from 12–15 poplar-wood planks around 10 mm thick that were glued edge-to-edge. Gone were the sophisticated multi-layer plywood strips of the earlier shields. Gone, too, was the expensive brass edging, instead rawhide, that tough-but-flexible inner layer of cowskin, was used to edge the oval shields. Iron or copper-alloy bosses found at Dura and across the empire, were fitted over a pair of holes cut into the board to accept the owner's fingers and thumb. Providing an essential handgrip and also helping to bind the planks of the board together was an iron bar that crossed longitudinally, it was riveted through the shield board at either end.

The shields all seem to have been slightly 'dished', curving gently and uniformly back from the shield boss. Shield 633, however, was an exception. It was a fragment (now lost) of a broad oval shield, but it was constructed from the same sort of plywood as the traditional, rectangular *scutum*. It is possible that plywood was swapped for a plank-type construction in order to effect the 'dishing' seen in the majority of shields. Plywood can be bent easily in a single direction but not at all in two or more directions simultaneously. Clearly, at least some of the broad, oval shields of the third century were made of plywood like shield 633 and were therefore flat.[10]

Surprisingly, these shields were every bit as large, heavy and encumbering as their rectangular forebears. The best preserved examples have a height between 107 and 118 cm and a width between 92 and 97 cm. Compare these measurements with the old-style rectangular shield also dug up at Dura which had a height of 102 cm and a width of 83 cm.

Oval shields had been used by the Roman auxiliary troops for several centuries, but those shields were much narrower than the third century type. Although there are no complete auxiliary shields available to study, two leather shield covers were found at Valkenburg in Germany. One was for a tall, oval shield and the other for a shorter shield with parallel sides and curved ends. Both are assumed to be for auxiliary use. The leather cover for the oval shield is 130 cm by 65 cm, the shorter cover is 100 cm by 53 cm. At least two or three centimetres needs to be taken away from these measurements to take account of the cover's need to fold-over. Remains of an auxiliary shield-board found at Doncaster, England, were of a laminated, multi-layer construction, much like the known curved legionary shields. Plainly, these and the many auxiliary shields of similar dimensions from Trajan's Column, are not the same as the plank-built, broad ovals found at Dura and on third century tombstones.

An interesting feature on some inner faces of the Dura shield boards was a fastening loop on the upper left. This has been interpreted as an attachment for a strap, allowing the soldier to carry the shield over his shoulder. Reconstructions by the author have shown this to be a great benefit on long marches, or when the wearer's hands need to be freed for other tasks. In 2006 the author conducted an 18 km walk along the highest parts of Hadrian's Wall carrying reconstructed third century armour and equipment. Negotiating the steep and sometimes rocky terrain required one hand free while the other held a spear. The shield was carried on the back, held there by a leather strap that was attached to a brass ring much like those found on the Dura examples.

Shields at Dura were covered with a layer of rawhide faced with linen cloth and this enabled them to be painted. Studies have shown a remarkable break in tradition between the shield designs of the second century and those of the third. The famous Roman motifs of thunderbolts and wings that adorn the shields of legionaries on Trajan's Column and a number of tombstones, are noticeably absent from the Column of Marcus Aurelius and onwards throughout the third century.

The Dura shields vary in decoration. The most striking is a portrait of an eastern warrior god, painted on a green background and clutching a spear and shield (a broad oval shield, of course!). Two of the Dura shields depict, in intricate detail, a host of warriors ready for battle. These are the 'Homeric shield' and the 'Amazon shield', the figures were painted onto a dark red background, and were thought to be so elaborate as to mark the shields out as non-combat parade items. They may actually have been used by cavalry for their colourful 'sports' manoeuvres where teams of horsemen split into Greeks and Amazons. Most shield backs are uniformly painted, but that of the 'Amazon shield' (shield 617) has a unique paint-job, a blue field is decorated with a radial pattern of eight spokes, each spoke made up of several heart-shaped motifs in white. A single star is placed between each spoke. Simon James, who excavated at Dura Europus, believes this design may actually be a unit insignia, normally found painted on the face of a shield. Both 'Amazon' and 'Heroic' shield designs featured border decoration, and this border decoration is also found on a number of other shield fragments.

In both construction and decoration, the Dura designs *seem* totally unrelated to any earlier Roman shield. In fact there is a point of connection, both with earlier auxiliary shields and also with some of the designs featured within the later fourth century list of regiments: the Notitia Dignitatum. Lost in the desert between Persia and Rome, these shields link the early imperial tradition with the Late Roman. Obvious similarities include wreath-like bands around the central boss that harken back to laurel crowns and victory wreaths, as well as heart-shaped or ivy motifs and stars. Was the broad oval simply a development of the auxiliary shield? These decorative clues suggest an auxiliary heritage rather than a legionary or even a foreign one. There are of course fragments of legionary rectangular *scuta* at Dura and remarkably they too are decorated in a style reminiscent of auxiliary shields from the first and second centuries. The complete example features a square-shaped wreath-like band around the boss , with an eagle flanked by winged figures above it, and a lion below it. Stars flank this lion. Trajan's Column, a century and a half earlier, boasts several shields displaying these decorative elements including stars, wreaths, animals standing alone below the boss, eagles sitting alone above it.

Comparative analysis of the Dura shield designs with earlier auxiliary patterns could lead to various conclusions. One of them, certainly, is that Roman troops modified the existing auxiliary shield for use by both the auxiliaries *and* the legions. Why this was must relate to the simultaneous adoption of longer sword types such as the 'Lauriacum-Hromowka'.

Why?

Fashion may explain changes in sword hilt, in types of clothing or in brooch styles, but when it comes to offensive and defensive equipment, tactical and practical needs are paramount. If the rectangular shield and *gladius* represent a tightly packed and close-in style of combat, what does the pairing of the broad, oval shield and long *spatha* represent?

It is likely that the 'Antonine revolution', the change in shield shape, helmet type and the switch from *pilum* to spear, was fuelled by a need for longer swords. Just like the cavalry, the infantry needed a weapon with greater reach in order to tackle the increasing numbers of mounted opponents they were meeting on the battlefield. Sarmatian tribes played a significant role in the Marcomannic Wars and passed on their horsemanship to some of the German tribes. Goths sweeping into Europe from southern Russia were mounted, as were the Parthians and their aggressive successors, the Persians. This move to a longer sword had other repercussions.

Given the longer sword type, a change in the shape of the shield is understandable. The back projecting corners of the rectangular legionary shield are a serious hindrance in sword combat using a *spatha*, as sparring sessions conducted by the author with reconstructed weaponry have demonstrated. While thrusting attacks with the *spatha* proved easy enough, slashing blows aimed at a defending opponent proved extremely difficult. Switching to the new-style broad oval shield, the cutting attacks were more easily made, the curve of the shield allowing both vertical and diagonal strikes. Simon James calls this new combination a 'tactical package'.[11]

Part of the new package was the use, by legionaries and auxiliaries alike, of spears. *Auxilia* had always used spears with their narrow oval shields – legionaries, however, did not. The spear rests happily at the upper right corner of an oval shield and can be handled aggressively in combat within that 'zone'. The rectangular shield of the legions has a sharp corner in this 'zone', forcing the spearman to either hold his weapon along the side of the *scutum* or along its top edge. Neither of these choices comfortably allows an attack capable of striking over the opponents' shield whilst still keeping one's own shield raised high in a defensive posture.

A transformation in the style of Roman helmets also contributed to this 'tactical package'. As chapter 6 explains, these new helmets featured very deep neck guards that prevented their wearers from adopting a crouched stance. The *gladius*-like stabbing attacks into the abdomen of enemy soldiers were simply not possible with the introduction of these helmets. The evidence points instead to an upright fighting stance, with the longer sword used for cutting and slashing attacks as well as thrusts to the head, chest and sides of an opponent.

Individual fencing styles may have been catered for by the two types of *spatha* on offer in the third century, but either type, Straubing or Lauriacum, was capable of both types of attack. Vegetius, writing around AD 400 described how recruits training with the *spatha* 'learned to strike not with the edge, but with the point... a stab driven two inches in is fatal; for necessarily whatever goes in penetrates the vitals. Secondly while a cut is being delivered the right arm and flank are exposed;' In a similar vein, Ammianus Marcellinus, an officer in the mid-fourth century, relates how the usurper Silvanus was butchered with 'sword thrusts' from Roman *spatha*.

Whilst Vegetius urged the soldier to thrust with the sword, it is certain that the *spatha* could also be used to slash. Ammianus Marcellinus, records that at the battle of Strasbourg, 'the hail of darts and javelins and the volleys of iron-tipped arrows did not slacken, although blade was clashing on blade in hand-to-hand conflict,' A few years later, pursuing the Persian forces outside the walls of Ctesiphon in AD 363, emperor Julian's light-armed troops are reported to be 'hacking at the backs and legs of the Persians and their monstrous (elephants) as they turned tail.'

Again Ammianus, a retired Roman officer of some experience, painted an evocative picture of Gothic casualties on the field of Adrianople: 'Our men were too close-packed to have any hope of escape; so they resolved to die like heroes, faced the enemy's swords, and struck back at their assailants... You might see a lion-hearted (Goth), who had been hamstrung or had lost his right hand or been wounded in the side, grinding his clenched teeth and casting defiant glances around in the very throes of death.' Note the two types of wound received from Roman *spatha*, first the cut which had sliced off Gothic hands and the stab wounds into the sides of the barbarians' torsos.[12]

If the Roman soldier had been content with a thrusting weapon he would surely have stuck with the *gladius*. As it was he had migrated to the *spatha*, a multi-functional weapon equally capable of both modes of attack. Both modes were undoubtedly employed on the battlefield. 'The emphasis was most definitely "cut" and thrust,' writes the historian Ian Stephenson, 'as opposed to the earlier "thrust" and cut.'[13]

6

Battlefield Protection

'Have no fear whatever of the Romans; for they are superior to us neither in numbers nor in bravery. And here is the proof: they have protected themselves with helmets and breastplates and greaves ... for they are influenced by their fears when they adopt this kind of fighting in preference to the plan we follow of rough and ready action.'

Dio Cassius 62.5

It was late August in 55 BC and Julius Caesar was in command of a small invasion force heading directly for a shingle beach at Deal, north of Dover. Two legions of infantry were about to put ashore in a bid to gain a victory for Caesar against the native tribes of Britain. Those tribes were lined up on the beach ready and waiting to oppose the landing. Caesar, in his own account of the expedition, explains how his soldiers refused to disembark from the transports to brave both the North Sea surf as well as the British army. The standard-bearer of Legion X Equestris called on the troops around him and leapt from the ship to wade ashore alone, shaming (or spurring on) his comrades to join him. A fierce battle on the shore-line followed, but it was Caesar's legionaries who prevailed eventually forcing the alliance of tribes to retreat to safety further inland. The two legions made such an impact on the assembled British tribes that the chiefs soon sent envoys back to Deal to sue for peace.

It was a peace that would not last and Caesar, despite a second expedition a year later, could not exploit the precarious toe-hold he had gained in Britain. Yet his legionaries had shocked the British warriors with that first encounter. In AD 43, almost a hundred years later, general Aulus Plautius would repeat Caesar's invasion with far greater success. Relentlessly, in battle after battle, the Roman soldier seemed to prevail against his British foe, despite a fierce native resistance.

In the eyes of the Britons, a tribal warrior was one of the elite, a nobleman owning lands and cattle and round-houses. For most of these warriors who were themselves retainers of the chiefs, keen to win glory and fame in war, their fighting kit would have consisted of a sword, a shield and a spear. There was no protection to be had other than that offered by the gods or the ritual magic granted by arcane symbols painted on bare skin with blue woad. Some, probably only the richest of the tribal aristocrats, would own a shirt of ringmail and perhaps a helmet.

For the tribal levies, the farmers and herdsman who had followed their chiefs to Deal with only an iron-tipped spear and a shield, the sight of thousands of legionaries wading ashore must have been shocking. Every single Roman soldier was dressed as elaborately, and in many cases more elaborately, than their own wealthy chiefs. Caesar had brought with him an army of chieftains to face the unarmoured but strong-hearted warriors of Britain.

The Helmet

Just as the design of swords developed and changed due to a mix of fashion and battlefield necessity, helmets too evolved. Those bold legionaries leaping ashore with Julius Caesar in 55 BC wore bronze Monteforino or Coolus helmets, plain and unadorned, with short neck guards and few reinforcements. A hundred years on and troops from Claudius' AD 43 invasion of Britain were sporting a development of the Coolus, a type labelled by H. Russell Robinson as the Imperial-Gallic. This iron helmet is traditionally associated with the Roman soldier. It featured cut-outs for the ears, a heavy brow strip, a lower and wider neck guard, more substantial cheek guards, decoration in the form of small brass roundels and a prominent 'eyebrow' design.[1]

It seems that the Dacians depicted on Trajan's Column valiantly defending their homelands against the legions, may have had some influence on the design of Roman helmets. Dacian warriors used a two-handed blade, called a falx, that was unique to these people. It had a devastating impact on the legions. The falx was adopted as the national weapon of the Dacians, in the same way that the kukri has become a recognised symbol of the Ghurkas. More than a century after the defeat and Romanisation of Dacia in AD 106, cohors I Aelia Dacorum Milliaria was recruited from the region and sent to the remote fort of Birdoswald on Hadrian's Wall. The cohort commander, Marcus Claudius Menander, erected a dedication stone and, next to the Latin inscription, is a carving of a curved Dacian falx. Dacia was now a settled Roman province, yet its men still revered the falx, perhaps as a symbol of their martial identity.[2]

Almost a two-handed sword, the *falx* may have split open Roman helmets of the day, forcing armourers in camp to hastily consider reinforcing the helmets of the legions. Some of the helmets are shown on Trajan's Column with thin bars of cross-bracing across the crown, 'hot-cross bun style'. From the years immediately following the Dacian Wars come a few fragmentary examples of Imperial-Gallic helmets that have been retrofitted with this new type of reinforcement. One can equate the plight of legionaries, desperately welding cross-bracing onto their Imperial-Gallic helmets, with soldiers throughout history. In the Vietnam War, drivers of the M113 armoured personnel carrier had their controls extended out the top-hatch so they could sit on the top of the vehicle. In this way they might survive when the M113 ran over a Viet Cong mine. In the First World War, raids on enemy trenches created the need for close-quarter weapons that the British Army had never foreseen. 'Trench clubs' were made by carpenters behind the lines out of wooden batons, made lethal by weighting with lead, hollowed-out Mill's Bombs or rows of hammered hobnails. In response, the German high command issued many of the storm troopers preparing for the Western Front's March 1918 Offensive with articulated steel body armour (the *Infantrie-Panzer*).

Cross-bracing may have been added as an after-thought to the Imperial-Gallic helmet of the Dacian Wars. However, in the early decades of the second century, a variation of this popular helmet was beginning to gain popularity within the legions. Robinson called this type the Imperial-Italic, since he believed it to be an inferior Italian-manufactured version of the Gallic. The early versions certainly lacked the fine finish of the Imperial-Gallic although it did adhere to the same principles and looked very similar.

This type of helmet continued to be developed during the reign of Hadrian, Antoninus Pius and Marcus Aurelius. Several beautifully decorated examples have been discovered with brass motifs applied to the helmet bowl, neck guard and cheek-plates. An Imperial-Italic G, for example, was found at Hebron in Israel. It featured riveted cross-bracing on the crown and brass crescent moons interspersed between them. Another example (Imperial-Italic D) from Mainz on the Rhine frontier, was embellished with motifs of brass temples and altars as well as a large imperial eagle. These Italic D helmets incorporated flat bands of brass reinforcement over the crown which predate the Dacian Wars. It may be that they fared well against the *falx*, inspiring wearers of the Gallic type to consider retrofitting iron cross-bracing to their own helmets.

The pinnacle of Roman helmet design came with the Imperial-Italic H helmet, of which a stunning example was found at Niedermörmter in Germany. Another famous example (origin unknown) was held in the Axel Guttman collection. Both of these helmets feature sturdy brow guards, very broad neck guards, elaborate embossing and applied, beaded decoration. As the author can attest, they are big and encumbering helmets to wear, yet they still look recognisably Roman.

By AD 200 Roman infantry soldiers had abandoned the Imperial-Italic tradition. Some 'H' designs may have continued in use into the third century, but the preferred helmet type was one already in use by the cavalry. These helmets look very different from the Imperial types; they are all-enclosing, without ear holes and leaving only a narrow 'T-shaped' opening for the face. The brow band is pointed and accentuated and the formidable cross-bracing stands on-edge for greater strength. The biggest difference by far is the placement of the neck guard. The newly adopted cavalry helmets had a bowl that did not stop at the neck as had been the case with the earlier Imperial designs, instead they plunged all the way down to the base of the neck. They literally sat on the legionary's shoulders.

These helmets have been labelled the 'Niederbieber' type by archaeologists after a distinctive all-iron example found at a military site on the Rhine. A similar iron helmet with brass fittings was found at Heddernheim, near Frankfurt. Rainau-Buch, north of Aalen in southern Germany was the site of yet another type made of copper-alloy. Known as the Buch helmet, it did not have the vertical cross-bracing of the Niederbieber and was dated to around 260. Cheek-pieces of the Buch design have also been recovered from Dura Europus, Britain and other sites in Germany. The scholar H. Russell Robinson categorised them as Auxiliary Cavalry Type E helmets.

1

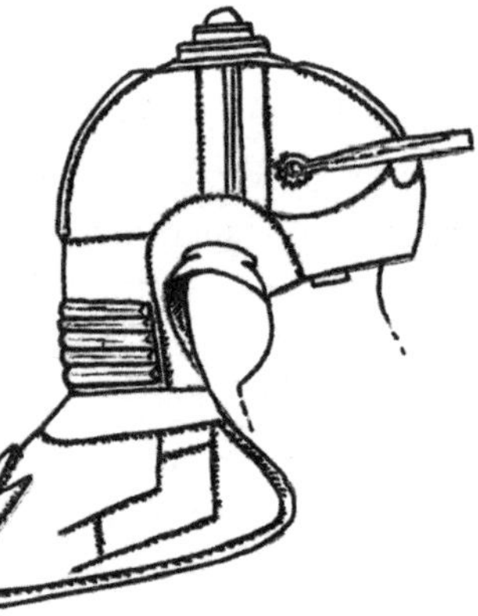

2

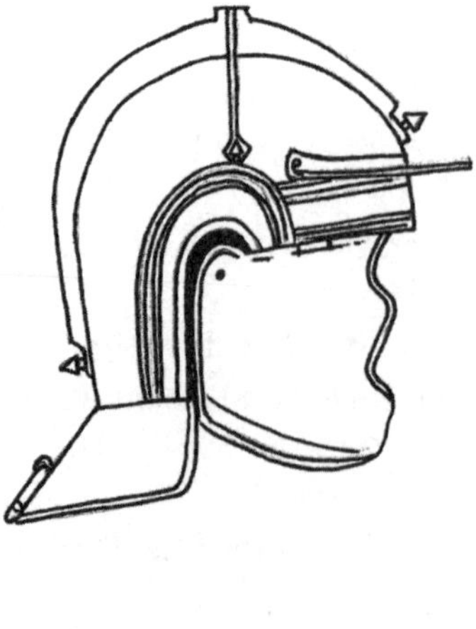

Third century helmets. 1 Niedermörmter (Imperial-Italic H); 2 Heddernheim. (*after Michael Simkins*)

Wearing a Niederbieber, one finds out quickly enough that visibility and hearing are restricted; in addition any attempt to look 'up' is futile since the helmet sits squarely on the shoulders. A crouching stance, favoured by soldiers from Trajan's legions, is virtually impossible – instead one has to stand upright and fight over the top of the shield. It is not just the modern re-enactor that finds the Niederbieber uncomfortable and restrictive. Sextus Julius Africanus, writing in the early third century, recorded the complaints of soldiers griping about the difficulty they had moving their heads while wearing the helmets of the day. He says the helmets:

> offer not enough protection against sling-shots, provide too little room for breathing and vision, and by extending down to the shoulder blades, they restrict the movement of the head. Thus in battle the Roman soldier not only suffers injury from sling-shots, but he cannot see incoming missiles or, if he does, the helmet cutting around his neck inhibits turning the head and dodging the projectiles.[3]

Roman infantrymen killed in a siege mine beneath Tower 19 at Dura Europus were found clad in ringmail armour and with their broad oval shields, but without their helmets. This was almost certainly because the crouched fighting stance required in the tunnel skirmishes made the Niederbieber a liability.

It could be argued that it was the nature of the new helmets that forced a change in the legionary's fighting stance and the shift to a long sword and oval shield. However, the reverse is more likely. With the adoption of the long *spatha* and the oval shield, legionaries were now fighting over the tops of their shields thus enabling them to take advantage of the cavalry's all-enclosing and heavily armoured Niederbieber helmet.

Ringmail

> And there marched on either side twin lines of infantrymen with shields and crests gleaming with glittering rays, clad in shining mail
>
> Ammianus Marcellinus 16.10

A popular misconception promulgated by the movies is that ancient warriors were defended by their armour. Shields, if carried at all, are recklessly cast aside after fighting begins in order for the actor to carry out the flamboyant sword-fighting display taught to him by the stunt co-ordinator. In truth the shield bore the brunt of an opponent's attack, a warrior without a shield was defenceless. Armour acted more as a last-ditch defence, a just-in-case back-up should that blow get past the shield. Who would risk relying only on a layer of body armour

Ringmail from Thorsberg showing alternate rivetted and welded rings.

to ward off the extreme trauma and penetrating wound from a sharp iron bar brought down by an adrenalin-fuelled six-foot tall barbarian?

Ringmail (*lorica hamata*) is often associated with the Viking and later Medieval period, but this just indicates how long-lived and successful this type of armour was. It was constructed in the form of a shirt made of small iron rings that were linked together through two other rings directly above and below them. Roman mail armour was made up of rows of solid rings (welded shut or punched out of an iron sheet), alternating with rows of rings that have their ends riveted together. This time-consuming method of manufacture created an incredibly strong 'net' of iron rings that was extremely difficult to force open with fast-moving arrowheads or powerfully thrust spear-points.

Mail shirts found at Caerleon in Wales, South Shields in England, Dura Europus in Syria, Buch, Künzing and Bertoldsheim in Germany show a remarkable uniformity in the size of the iron rings used, with an empire-wide standard of 7 mm external diameter and 1 mm thickness. Many of the fragments recovered from Dura Europus featured copper-alloy edging rings in their design, and these were either stamped or butted together, never riveted) A number of the mail coats discovered from across the empire were found rolled up by their former owners. Just as helmets were transported in waterproof leather bags, there is evidence in *Maurice's Strategikon* that ringmail was rolled up, stored and carried in some sort of a cylindrical leather case. The experience of the author has shown that damp conditions will readily turn a carelessly stored shirt of chainmail orange with rust.

Ringmail was certainly able to prevent deep cuts from slashing blades, as well as the penetration of spears and arrows; but the massive trauma inflicted by a powerful blow during hand-to-hand combat would easily pass through a thin layer of metal rings. A solid strike from a *spatha*, or a spear, could easily break ribs and crack collar-bones, whether ringmail was worn or not. Consequently, a padded garment was worn beneath the armour. This *subarmalis* can sometimes be seen peeking out from beneath armour on wall-paintings and in mosaics of the period, but no physical examples have survived. It is likely that the *subarmalis* was constructed in linen (those depicted are white, which often denotes the use of undyed linen), either a score or more layers glued together, or two layers with wool packed between them and then quilted. Both create a viable 'dead space' behind the ringmail which provides that vital protection from blunt trauma.

An anonymous author and amateur military tactician from the later fourth century gives us more information. In his *De Rebus Bellicis* he tells us that the Roman legions use a padded garment 'to counteract the weight and friction of armour ... This type of garment is made of thick sheep's wool felt to the measure ... of the upper part of the human frame...' A body, probably that of a Persian infantryman, found at the Tower 19 mine of Dura wore a badly corroded ringmail shirt. Adhering to the rings was a material (possibly felt) that is thought to be the remains some form of *subarmalis*.[4]

> Now the sun had risen higher, and when it had finished its course... it scorched the Romans, who were more and more exhausted by hunger and worn out by thirst, as well as distressed by the heavy burden of their armour.
>
> Ammianus Marcellinus 31.13

Although heavy, a shirt of ringmail armour is very flexible. Ringmail shirts from the earlier imperial period were short-sleeved and waist-length but during the third century the shirts began to reach mid-thigh and down to the elbow or even wrist. Such shirts, containing many more rings in their makeup, were even heavier. Modern reconstructions (with short-sleeves) weigh around 10 kg, whilst examples featuring sleeves reaching down to mid-forearm weigh around 12 kg.

Heavy and durable though they were, shirts of *lorica hamata* were easy to manufacture. They were certainly time-consuming to make, but in a slave economy, that was of little concern. During the first century AD, ringmail would be eclipsed by the new *lorica segmentata*, the famous banded armour of the legions. Once this had faded from use, however, the *lorica hamata* once again began to dominate the shelves of Roman armouries.

Scale Armour

Lorica squamata, or scale, was made up of small metal plates that were sewn onto a linen or leather backing. The plates were usually of copper-alloy but iron scales are also known. Each scale was punctured with pairs of holes that enabled the manufacturer to sew the scales to the backing fabric, to their neighbours and also to a horizontal linen thread. Earlier scale was only sewn to a horizontal thread, and in this way resembled 'fish scale'. The leather backing also acted as an additional *subarmalis*, although a padded shirt may still have been required, particularly because this 'locked' or 'rigid' scale could not extend below the waist. Finds of scale from the third century are as common as iron rings from *lorica hamata* and the representational evidence in the third century suggests that both ringmail and scale armour were equally popular with the legions. A partial shirt of scale found at Carpow in Scotland and dated to the Severan period was made up of copper-alloy scales 15 mm long and 13 mm wide. These scales were pierced by six holes, two at the top and two more lower down on either edge. While some of the scales found at Dura Europus follow this pattern, others feature a set of four holes at the top, rather than two, or a single hole on the top edge. Other combinations were also found which indicates a great variation in styles of scale armour manufacture.

Polished or tinned bronze scale certainly looks impressive and is not as badly affected by damp as ringmail. In addition, the armour is easier to wear and much lighter than an equivalent-sized shirt of ringmail. Because the shirt is made rigid by the scales, it must include in its manufacture a full-length opening to allow the wearer to put it on. Once on, the scale shirt is fastened up with buckles. Most modern reconstructions place this vulnerable opening on the shield side, under the arm, where the seam cannot be exploited by an enemy thrust. Integral arms cannot be made into a suit of scale armour due to the inflexibility of the design, but separately made sleeves of scale can be attached with buckles and straps most successfully.

Squamata does have its drawbacks, however, which explains the historical survival of ringmail and scale together in the same army, the same legions, perhaps even in the same squads. On a practical level, threads can break when they get caught, scales can come off and gaps can appear in the armour. Where ringmail is durable and tough, yet prone to damp and rust, scale is light and comfortable, yet needs regular maintenance.

Locked scale armour was inflexible; with each plate wired to the backing and to its neighbours, there was no movement. The author has discovered that modern examples of locked scale ride up against the wearer's throat when a climb is attempted. In addition, the scales do not expand or contract like the rings of a *hamata* shirt, and this makes climbing uphill very difficult. When a deep breath is required, the scale refuses to expand and one can feel restricted and short of breath. The answer of course is to loosen the straps, but at the expense of opening up a split in the side of the scale suit.[5]

Lorica Segmentata

Trajan's legionaries are shown on the Column wearing a type of sheet metal armour called by archaeologists *lorica segmentata*. Semi-circular strips of iron bend around the wearer's torso to meet at back and front where they are fastened with leather ties. Shoulders are protected by more curved iron strips, diminishing in size from the neck across toward the upper arm. *Segmentata* was probably designed to protect the shoulders and chest from the downward blows from German and Celtic long swords; legs, arms and groin are all left unarmoured. This is the signature armour of the Roman soldier as depicted in books and movies. Yet it was never as widespread as *lorica hamata*, neither was it in use for as long. Fragments of *segmentata* can be dated to Augustan times, in the early first century and the latest finds provide a final date for the armour of around AD 260, well within the third century. Contrast that two hundred and fifty year period with that of *hamata* which was worn from the Punic Wars of the second century BC right through to the sixth century AD, a period in excess of six hundred years.

Throughout its history *lorica segmentata* was worn exclusively by the legionaries rather than the auxiliary troops. Explanations for this vary. It may have been to restrict unreliable auxiliaries to more inferior kit should a rebellion break out, it may have been to reduce costs, or it may have been simply because the kit was complex. Unlike ringmail, which was durable and tough, *segmentata* will have required extensive maintenance. It fell apart frequently and we know this because of the hinges, buckles and decorative bosses that are found on many legionary sites across the empire.

In an era of military transformation, the legions continued to use *lorica segmentata*, just as they continued with their use of ringmail and scale. It was tried and tested technology. Archaeologists have worked hard to piece together the fragments of *segmentata* found in the ground. Inspired by artistic representations of the armour found on columns of Trajan and Marcus Aurelius, scholars have created working reconstructions. A metalworker's hoard found at Corbridge, south of Hadrian's Wall in 1964, provided scholars like H. Russell Robinson with two sets of the armour that proved crucial to perfecting a reconstruction. On one set, leather straps secured by buckles attached the chest hoops to the iron shoulder plates – this design became known as the Corbridge type A. The second set had dispensed with straps and instead was fitted with brass hooks that secured the shoulder plates to the torso section. This was named the Corbridge B and was assumed to be an improved development of the Corbridge A. The Corbridge hoard as a whole was dated to Hadrian's reign.

An attempt to simplify the *segmentata* was made in the mid-second century. This 'Newstead' type would be the design used throughout the third century. Aurelius Alexianus, a Spartan serving with Caracalla (*c.* 212-17), for example, is depicted on his gravestone wearing *lorica segmentata* beneath a cloak. On the Arch of Septimius Severus at Leptis Magna, a range of armour is depicted, including examples of lorica segmentata [6]

Reconstructions of *segmentata* are lighter, at 9 kg, than a shirt of ringmail. When worn with a padded *subarmalis* they are fairly comfortable and allow easy

ΜΑΡΚΟΣ
ΑΥΡΗΛΙΟΣ
ΑΛΕΖΥΣΘΕΩΝΣ
ΣΤΡΑΤΕΥΣΑ
ΜΕ ΝΟΣ
ΚΑΤΑΠΕΡΣΩΝ
ΕΤΗ ΒΙΩΣΑΣ
Λ

Tombstone of Aurelius Alexianus, from Athens. (*after Steven Richardson*)

movement since arms and legs are not restricted. Defence-wise the overlapping iron plates provide great strength and rigidity and must surely have soaked up a large amount of trauma damage that the more flexible mail would have let through.

Sets of the Corbridge type may have survived well into the third century. Reuse and reconditioning of equipment was a standard feature of the arms and armour supply within the Roman military. Since there was never an official set of kit, anything serviceable seems to have continued in use despite the prevalence of newer designs or fashions. If it worked it was used, if it was damaged it was repaired, if beyond repair it was replaced. *Segmentata* is known to have been in use for at least until 260, parts of Newstead *segmentata* were discovered at Carlisle, in England, as well as the fort of Zugmantel in Germany which was in use until that date. Excavations at León in Spain have produced finds that suggest that *segmentata* may have continued in use into the late third century and perhaps even beyond.[7]

A great 'rationalisation' of the Roman military occurred after AD 284 and it is probable that *lorica segmentata* became one of the victims of that process. Simplification, coupled with drastic money saving measures became the top priority of the new emperor. *Lorica segmentata*, expensive to manufacture and difficult to maintain, had to go. Those sets that were still serviceable probably continued to be used, but it is likely that this rationalisation ended production for good.

Greaves

Another form of body armour had always been utilised by the Roman legions to some extent over the previous centuries; it was leg armour, commonly known as greaves (*ocrea*). In the earlier imperial period it seems the centurions wore a set of bronze or iron greaves and these were often decorated. By AD 100 and possibly earlier, leg protection was becoming popular amongst other ranks. Some of the soldiers depicted on the Tropaeum Traiani at Adamclissi are shown wearing greaves and none of these soldiers appear to represent centurions. In the third century soldiers are shown on wall-paintings at Dura Europus wearing greaves and part of a copper-alloy example was actually recovered from the site. Iron greaves are known from Hebron as well as Künzing in Germany. This type of armour protected the shins from ankle to just below the knee. They were folded around the front and sides of the lower leg, and attached with straps of leather. The *Strategikon*, a valuable fifth century manual on Roman warfare, recommended that front-rank legionaries wear greaves. They were essential for the soldiers at the front of the formation whose shields were not big enough to protect shins unless the order was given for the frontline to kneel and ground its shields. *See* Colour Plate 18.

> The picked men of the files should have mail coats, all of them if it can be done... They should also have iron ... greaves, at least the first and last soldier in each file.
>
> Maurice, *Strategikon, 12.4.*

The author has manufactured iron greaves based on the Künzing model and found that even a fairly thin iron sheet can still protect the shins adequately from moderate trauma. After being cut to shape, the greave is bent down its centre giving a line of strength that faces forward. The greave is then gently and repeatedly bent to form a comfortable fit around the lower leg. Both upper and lower edges are 'turned' in order to prevent the edge of the greave digging into the skin. Padding is essential, and thick leg wraps or a padded layer of cloth wrapped or tied around the lower leg, serves this purpose well.

The treasure trove of artefacts recovered from Dura Europus includes a single fabric pad for a greave. Made of stout linen (around 0.5 cm thick) and with six ties for fastening around the lower leg, the padding would have provided that cushioning effect behind a metal greave. It is the only textile example known to us, although a leather pad for backing a greave was found at Vindonissa in Germany. Padding of leather, felt or linen was normally worn behind the greaves.

Manicae

It had once been thought that the Dacian *falx* had forced Roman soldiers to adopt metal defences for the right (sword) arm during Trajan's Dacian Wars. However, arm-guards (*manicae*) predate the Dacian Wars, as two tombstones from Mainz indicate. Sextus Valerius Severus and Gaius Annius Salutus were both from Legio XXII, a unit which was at Mainz in Germany between AD 43–70. The protection depicted on the Tropeum Traiani at Adamclissi actually resembles the segmented armguard worn by gladiators fighting in the arena and may have had its origins there. Confirmation of the design came with the finds of iron *manicae* fragments found at Carlisle dating to the Hadrianic period. More armguards were discovered at Carnuntum (Germany) as well as Newstead in Scotland, and these dated from the later mid-second century which certainly demonstrates the long-lasting appeal of the *manica* with the legions. *See* Colour Plate 19.

It is likely that *manicae* continued to be worn into battle by some Roman troops in the third century. A legionary on the Leptis Magna Arch of Septimius Severus certainly wears one, and a single iron segment from a *manica* was uncovered at Dura Europus. The sword arm is always at risk from slashing attacks by the enemy since it must of necessity be extended out from behind the shield's protection. Ammianus Marcellinus describes the sight of a wounded Goth at the battle of Adrianople who had lost his right hand in just this way.[8]

New Styles of Armour

Alba Iulia, in Romania, was the location of a Roman sculpture find dated very broadly to the late second or the early third century. Although not complete it does appear to show a legionary soldier clutching a curved rectangular *scutum*, the scabbard chape of his long *spatha* peeking out below the shield's lower rim. On his right arm is a segmented *manica* and toward his sternum (his head is missing) is a rectangular plate on top of scale armour. Although difficult to properly discern, this piece of scale armour appears to come from his right shoulder down past his throat to vanish behind the top of the *scutum*.

So what are we seeing here? *Manica*, *segmentata*, sword chape and *scutum* are all well defined and crisply detailed so that there is little doubt that the Alba Iulia legionary represents something real. The rectangular plate sitting on the

Legionary with curved shield and *segmentata*, from Alba Iulia, Romania. (*after M. Daniels*)

upper chest is attested in archaeological contexts. Associated with both ringmail shirts and scale armour, these twin iron or copper-allow plates sat at the top of the sternum and are curved on their upper edge to follow the curve of the neck. These throat plates were fastened together by a square-headed pin and often embossed with mythological scenes. Examples of chest-plates come from Bertoldsheim, Manching and elsewhere, with the Bertoldsheim plate found still attached to its ringmail shirt. They may have served as closures, used to tighten the *hamata*, as decorative pieces or simply as an additional layer of armour over a particularly vulnerable spot. *See* Colour Plate 20.

The Alba Iulia figure boasts a rectangular breast-plate over a section of scale armour. Some academics believe this scale to be an integral part of a revolutionary new type of composite *segmentata*. However, it is more likely to be a gorget, a circle of bronze scales sewn to a textile backing, with a hole at the centre through which the head can fit. The rectangular plates on the throat may be the closure device for this gorget. It may be distant in time, but a gorget of this style was discovered in Derveni, Greece and dated to the fourth century BC. Whilst it opened at the back, it could be tightened around the neck with the integral pull-ties.

Alternatively the tantalising view of scale armour on the Alba Iulia carving may represent the lower part of a coif, a form of head protection more associated with the Medieval knight. Coifs are a balaclava-like head-gear made up of ringmail or scales, sitting on a padded hood, with only the face showing. *See* Colour Plate 12. None have been found, but Roman soldiers on the later fourth century Vergillius Vaticanus manuscript are shown wearing them. Back in the third century soldiers representing Philistines on the 'Battle of Ebenezer' fresco at Dura Europus likewise wear coifs, either of ringmail or, more probably, scale. Whether these Philistines are modelled after Romans or Persians is unknown, however.

The trend was for ever more armour. Larger, more enclosing helmets were being worn by the infantry, ringmail sleeves often reached the elbow or wrist and were increasingly hanging down to mid-thigh. Arms and legs were always vulnerable; the use of iron or copper-alloy greaves and *manicae* aimed to address that vulnerability. Shirts of scale or ringmail could sometimes feature rectangular plates for additional protection of the upper chest, and it is likely that scale gorgets were also available to some troops. At no other period in Roman history, before or after, was the legionary so well protected and heavily armoured.

Soldiers wearing coifs, from the fourth century Vergillius Vaticanus. (*after Coulston*)

7

Other Weapons

'For it is not fine raiment or stores of gold, silver and gems that bend our enemies to respect or support us; they are kept down solely by fear of our arms.'

Vegetius 1.13

For centuries the Roman legionary had won or lost his battles with the sword – he was a swordsman. However, there were other weapons within the Roman arsenal: the spear, the javelin, the bow and the sling. All had their tactical role, used at the appropriate time against the appropriate opponent.

The Spear

Spears are one of the oldest and most ubiquitous weapons of the ancient world. Essentially a dagger on a long pole, the spear is able to reach forward to strike at an enemy's body while enabling the spearman to stand back, reducing his chance of injury. Since only the spearhead is iron, the weapon is cheap and an army can be equipped with spears quite affordably. Many armies in the past specialised in spear-fighting, none more so than the ancient Greek hoplites. Although they also carried a short sword, it acted only as a sidearm, a back-up weapon. Hoplites trained to fight and defeat an opposing army using their spears only, in this they differed radically from the legionary.

During the second century spears were a weapon more associated with auxiliary troops, men who fought with oval shields. In the third century spears certainly did become part of the legionary's repertoire. Now that the legionary shield was a broad oval, spears were as easy to use in combat as long swords, a flexibility that could be taken advantage of. The ancient writer Herodian praises the legions of Caracalla for their prowess with the spear: 'The Romans had an infantry force which was invincible in close-quarter fighting with spears,'[1]

Spears begin to appear on gravestones and wall paintings at the start of the third century but they never fully replaced the heavy legionary javelin, the *pilum*. This shock throwing weapon had been a part of the legions' armoury since its earliest days and it continued in use throughout the third century. The spear did not eclipse it, but instead, may have replaced it for certain types of battlefield engagement. It was the *pilum*, not the spear, that remained the essential weapon of front-rank legionaries during this period. By the fourth century, after Diocletian's 'rationalisation' of the Roman military, the *pilum* was replaced by a variety of lighter versions and the spear was universally adopted. This later period saw the development of sophisticated spear-fighting tactics. Formations such as the *foulkon* and *cuneus*, and a complete system of spear drill is described in detail by the ancient writer Maurice in the *Strategikon* and Ian Stephenson characterises the fourth century legionary as a close-quarter spearman, a 'return to the hoplite'.[2]

The length of these spears is not known for certain, but may have ranged between 2 – 2.7 metres. Spear heads were often long and leaf shaped, designed to penetrate deeply, cut muscle and rend internal organs with their long slicing blades. Each spear shaft terminated in a ferrule, a sharp iron spike, that was used to plant the spear in the ground during rest periods, or during periods of javelin throwing, but that was also used to spear defenceless or wounded foes that were being trampled underfoot. Spear shafts may have been decorated from the third century onwards with spirals of colour running along them. In addition some

Socketed spearhead from Künzing. (*after K.R. Dixon*)

of the spear shafts found in Danish bog deposits were decorated with intricate carvings just below the head and it is possible that Roman soldiers carved their spear shafts, too.

Used in massed formation, the spear proved to be an exceptionally efficient weapon. A static unit of infantrymen, with shields and spears, bristling outwards like the spikes of a sea urchin are of great defensive value on their own. Cavalry find a wall of spears and shields very intimidating and infantry units are wary of advancing on Roman spearmen, unless they have long spears themselves with which to reach their enemy. That is the great advantage of the spear over other weapons, it has great defensive value and if used in conjunction with other members of the unit is able to keep an attacker well beyond arm's length.

Spears can be used over-arm to stab down onto a foe, over his shield, but to do this the spear must be held near to the mid-point and is greatly foreshortened. In addition to losing the great advantage of the spear (its length) attacking over-arm presents a spearman's right arm, armpit and right chest to the attacker. Better is the under-arm spear thrust. The spear is held closer to the butt, which tucks under the forearm. Held like this the spear is stabbed powerfully forward into an enemy without exposing oneself to attack. It also allows better control of the spear shaft for raking aside an enemy spear, or for parrying the spear thrust of a foe. *See* Colour Plates 21, 22 and 23.

Reconstructions of spear and shield fighting methods have shown that the spear is effective when used in a dense formation although of course any modern reconstruction cannot do justice to the power and lethality of these weapons. Any form of weapon re-enactment is bound by strict safety rules, but it is clear that the most vulnerable targets open to a spear-wielding legionary are the face, throat and shins of an enemy warrior – exactly those areas of the body strictly off-limits as target areas in modern battle re-enactments. The author participated in an experiment to recreate two legionary battle-lines coming into contact. Prior to the two shield-walls slamming together, the (blunted) spear-points slid off of the shield boards and everyone involved had to keep their heads down to avoid getting a spear-point in the face. One participant was unlucky enough to receive a very minor cut to the cheek. Spear-points also slid down towards the shins and feet, though with much less danger of serious injury. The experiment brought home the very dangerous nature of spear and shield combat. Sharpened spear-points would obviously not slide as much but deflections off of the shield rim would achieve the same results.

The Javelin

> Only close up the ranks, and having discharged your javelins, then with shields and swords continue the work of bloodshed and destruction, without

a thought of plunder. When once the victory has been won, everything will be in your power.

Tacitus, *Annals 14.37*

Trajan's legions would not simply have marched into the Dacian hordes, shields at the ready and swords unsheathed ready for a fight. The *gladius* was the weapon that carried out the butcher work, but it was often used following a barrage of heavy javelins called *pila*. As the Roman front-line approached within 20 m of the enemy, the front ranks threw their *pila* and then drew their swords and charged.

Javelins had been employed throughout history. Traditionally they resembled very light spears, 1 – 1.5 m in length with a wooden shaft and small iron spearhead. Being light and fairly short these javelins could be thrown out to some distance and could be carried in bundles ready for delivering a volley.

The Roman *pilum* was different. Almost 2 m in length, only around half of this was composed of wooden shaft; a thin iron shank made up the top half of the weapon. On the tip of the soft iron shank sat an armour-piercing point of hardened iron, usually pyramidal in shape. In the third century these *pilum* shanks were connected to the wooden shaft either by a socket, a simple tang or a complex tang fixed with three iron rivets into a swelling of the wood at the joint. These were expensive javelins, heavy armour-piercing weapons used once and then (hopefully) recovered and reused once the battle had been won.

Legionaries carried one or two of these deadly armour and shield-piercing weapons and threw them at the enemy formation just prior to entering hand-to-hand combat. The aim was to hit an opponent and kill him, the pyramidal point, backed by the weight and momentum of the weapon, was designed to punch through armour to achieve this aim. Should it strike a shield the head could, when thrown with enough force, penetrate the shield board. The smooth iron shank allowed the head to slide through the shield to its full extent. The 'safe space' behind the shield was no longer safe since the *pilum* could potentially reach the man behind it. *See* Colour Plate 13. As a secondary benefit, any shield with a *pilum* in it was useless until it could be pulled out, certainly a job not feasible on the frontline of a formation about to go hand-to-hand with Roman legionaries. The *pilum* shanks bent easily out of shape and this may have been an unintended feature which was easy to remedy with a hammer, but which prevented the *pila* from being picked up and thrown back at the Roman line.

Other javelins of more traditional form, known as *lancea*, were commonly carried by light auxiliary troops and cavalry. These were cheaply made javelins, no more than a 1 metre wood shaft tipped with a simple leaf-shaped iron head. Auxiliary skirmish troops who had usually carried these javelins onto the battlefield were of far lower pay and status than the legionary. Yet in the late second and third centuries it seems that several legions may have begun to arm

1. Soldiers on the Column of Marcus Aurelius (AD 180). (*Author's collection*)

2. Arch of Septimius Severus in the Imperial Forum, Rome. (*Author's collection*)

3. *Above*: Part of a banquet scene on a wall painting from Komárom (Brigetio) in Hungary. (*Florian Himmler*)

4. *Left*: Husband and wife on a tombstone from Augsburg. (*Florian Himmler*)

5. *Below*: Painted tile depicting Heliodorus, a military accountant from Dura Europus. (*Yale University Art Gallery—Dura Europos Collection*)

6. *Above left*: Soldier 'out of armour'. (*Author's collection*)

7. *Above right*: Soldier in ringmail. (*Author's collection*)

8. *Below left*: Soldier in lorica segmentata. (*Author's collection*)

9. *Below right*: Lanciarius. (*Florian Himmler*)

10. *Above left*: Soldier with drawn spatha. (*Author's collection*)

11. *Above right*: Soldier in lorica squamata (*Author's collection*)

12. *Left*: Ringmail coif. (*Author's collection*)

13. *Above*: The penetrative power of a light pilum is tested against a rectangular scutum. (*Florian Himmler*)

14. *Right*: Scutum from Dura Europus (*Yale University Art Gallery—Dura Europos Collection*)

15. *Below*: Tribune Terentius leads the Dura garrison in a religious ceremony. (*Yale University Art Gallery—Dura Europos Collection*)

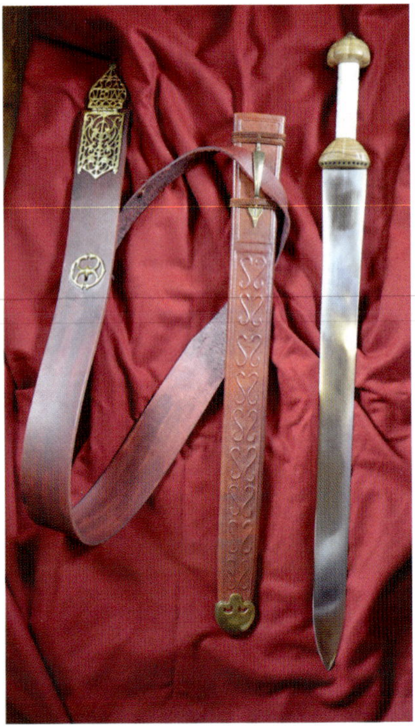

16. *Above left*: Baldric fitting. (*Author's collection*)

17. *Above right*: Reconstructed sword from Dura. (*Robert Mason*)

18. *Below*: A decorated copper-alloy greave from a private collection in Germany. (*Florian Himmler*)

19. Soldier wearing a brass manica on his sword-arm. (*Florian Himmler*)

20. Chest Plates. (*Author's collection*)

21. Spearman fighting overarm. (*Author's collection*)

22. Spearman fighting underarm. (*Author's collection*)

23. *Right*: Spearman, view from the front. (*Author's collection*)

24. *Below*: Main colonnaded street of Palmyra, Syria. (*Erik Hermans via Wikimedia Commons*)

25. Entrance to the hastily cut Roman counter-mine at Dura Europus. (*Marsyas via Wikimedia Commons*)

26. The western ('desert') wall of Dura Europus which the Persian army attempted to undermine. (*Erik Hermans via Wikimedia Commons*)

27. Sculpture at Naqsh-e Rostam, Iran, depicting the triumph of King Shapur I over the Roman Emperor Valerian. (*Ali Ganjei*)

28. Shapur I, King of Persia, on the face of a silver Sassanid coin. (*via Wikimedia Commons*)

29. The Aurelian Wall, commissioned by Emperor Aurelian after the Germanic invasions of Italy in 259 and 268. (*Author's collection*)

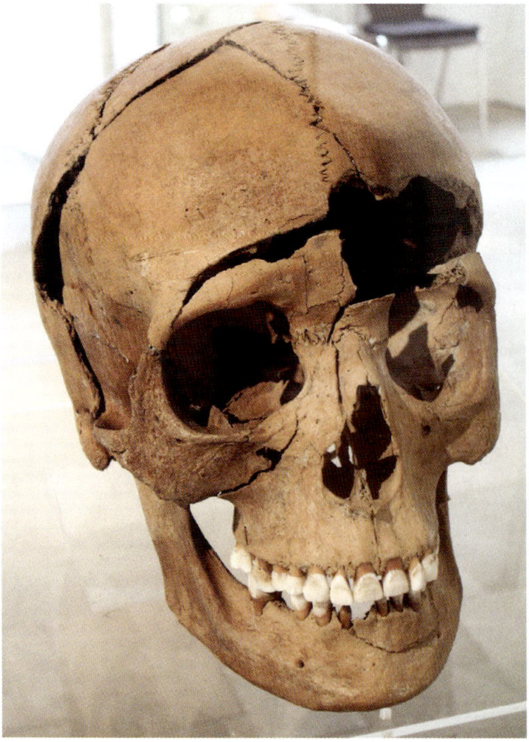

30. A victim of one Germanic attack at Regensburg-Harting in Germany. (*Florian Himmler*)

31. On Campaign: Roman soldiers as they might have looked in Germany and Dacia, on campaign against the Alemanni and Goths. Note the leather shield covers, the leg wrappings and heavy cloaks for warmth, as well as the leather bags needed to carry rations and personal belongings. (*Florian Himmler*)

32. Ludovisi Battle Sarcophagus: This exquisite marble sarcophagus may have been made for Hostilian, the son of Emperor Decius and dates to around 251. It depicts a furious battle between legionaries and German warriors. (*via Wikimedia Commons*)

Plates 33–35 on this page and plate 36 opposite top, show the standard military kit of the third century, complete with waterskin, cold-weather cloak (sagum), and goatskin bag. Finds of leather are rare—the bag is based on a find from the Comacchio shipwreck, which sank during the reign of Emperor Augustus.

37. Cavalry Helmet from the Third Century. This is a replica of a cavalry helmet from the third century found at Heddernheim, in Germany, decorated with bronze skinning. (*Author's collection*)

38. A collection of Roman arrowheads found on Hadrian's Wall, dating from the fourth century. (*Author's collection*)

39. These reproductions show the range of arrows available to the legions; these include socketed and tanged types, as well as trilobate bladed and bodkin-type armour piercing arrows. (*Author's collection*)

as many as 500 of their own number in this way for fast and mobile attacks. The new *lanciarii* troop type may have been something of an elite soldier. During Emperor Commodus' reign, for example, 1,500 'javelin men' from the three British legions were selected by their units to petition the emperor face-to-face in Rome. Late in the third century *lanciarii* from the legions were recruited as elite imperial guards.

Accounts tell of light infantry troops used in a skirmishing role, no doubt clutching handfuls of *lancea*, to harass enemy formations. At the battle of Nisibis in 217, for example, light troops belonging to the legions filled vulnerable gaps between the Roman lines and were standing by 'to make marauding forays' against the Parthians.[3]

Three gravestones belonging to some of these specialised *lanciarii* troops of II Parthica were found at Apamea, in Syria (dating to 215–218). Each man is shown clutching a bundle of short javelins. One soldier, Aurelius Mucianus, carries his javelins within a fabric or leather 'quiver' that would normally (one assumes) be slung over his shoulder. This would have allowed Mucianus and his comrades to keep up a barrage of javelins on the enemy force, or to easily pass the weapons forward to troops on the front-line. *See* Colour Plate 9.[4]

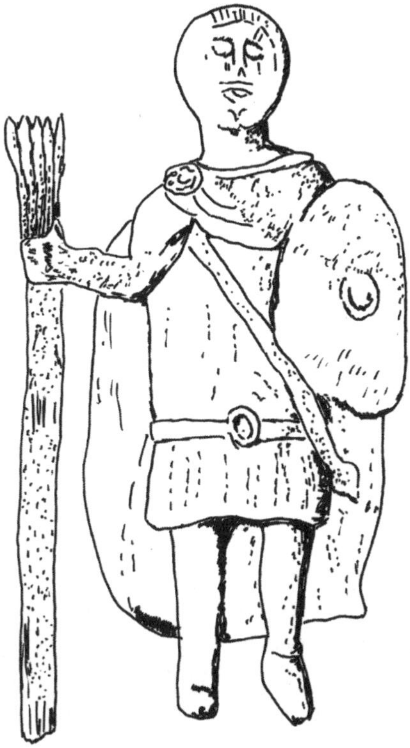

Tombstone of Aurelius Mucianus, *lanciarius*, from Apamea. (*after Bishop and Coulston*)

In practical terms, the javelin delivers a more powerful punch than the arrow or sling stone, but because of its size is in much shorter supply on the battlefield. Tests by the author with replica *lancea* have shown them to be unbalanced and accuracy is questionable at distances in excess of 15 m.

From Pilum to Spear

The move away from the *pilum* in the third century toward the new tactical combination of spear and javelin is just one more aspect of the radical transformation affecting the Roman military. Why were long spears being introduced into the Roman legion at the end of the second century? And how did that relate to the changes in sword and shield already discussed?

Spears have a particular defensive use against cavalry. In 135, the governor of Cappadocia, Lucius Flavius Arrianus Xenophon '(Arrian'), prepared the legionaries of XV Apollinaris and XII Fulminata to face a large cavalry force of Alans. He armed the first four ranks with *kontos* (in the Greek; almost certainly the Roman *hasta* or long spear) and the rear four ranks of legionaries with *lancea*. Arrian planned for the frontline to lower their spears and aim their tips at the horses' chests, hopefully dissuading them from charging into the formation. At the same time ranks 2–4 were to use their spears to wound the horses or kill their riders. Meanwhile the rear ranks were to begin a barrage of javelins over the heads of their comrades. When the Alans eventually give up their attack and retreat, the Roman formation was to open up to allow the Roman cavalry to begin the pursuit.[5]

Arrian's battle plan was probably not a one-off tactical innovation but more likely an accepted practice for certain situations. We have already seen that the Roman legions were facing more mounted foes than ever before. In the late second century, it may have seemed prudent to legionary commanders to have the capability to defend against cavalry tied into the legion on a more permanent basis.[6]

Infantry battles of the earlier period were often begun with volleys of *pila* being thrown until one side or the other closed with the sword. The greatest problem faced by a Roman legion was the way in which enemy cavalry could negate that devastating volley of *pila*. A cavalry charge was capable of closing with a Roman battle-line far more rapidly than could a formation of foot-soldiers. Now the amount of time between a cavalryman reaching *pilum* range and that horseman getting within infantry-killing range was very much reduced. The first two lines of Roman soldiers *may* have been able to cast a *pilum* at the enemy prior to contact but even that is doubtful, and then they would be facing charging horsemen armed only with a (short) sword.

We have already seen, in chapter 5, how the move to a long sword may have provided the longer reach needed against mounted opponents and that this required the use of an oval shield. The new-shaped shield also gave the legionary the ability to fight with a spear if necessary. By the time of Septimius Severus a new legionary model was developing and it may have been his prestigious II Parthica which pioneered this transformation. The gravestone inscriptions from Apamea not only record the existence of *lanciarii* within the legion but also *phalangiarii* (close-order spearmen). No record exists of what these *phalangiarii* did or how they were used.

Looking at Arrian's anti-cavalry preparations, it is easy to see a similar process occurring throughout the legions of the third century. Perhaps the first two or three ranks of a battlefield formation were armed with a spear, rather than the *pilum*, with this they would be able to fend off a cavalry charge just as the frontline of Arrian's legions were being ordered to do. While the spearmen kept the cavalry at bay, the rear ranks could pelt them with missiles. The heavy *pilum* would lack the range to easily clear the spearmen in front, but lighter javelins, such as the *lancea*, would do the job admirably. In the fourth century the heavy *pilum* disappears completely, to be replaced with a lighter version (the *spiculum*) and a heavy throwing dart (the *plumbata*). Both *spiculum* and *plumbata* were easily able to be thrown over the heads of front-line troops along with the ubiquitous light javelin. This trend toward the use of missile weapons that were able to be launched from behind the frontline, while it fought the enemy with spears, must have begun in the late second century.

What was being created then, and tested with Legio II Parthica, was a battle-line with both an offensive and a defensive capability. When the impetus of the cavalry charge had been broken, the infantry was then able to move forward using either spears or *spatha*. Alternatively, as happened at the battle of Emesa in 272, lightly-armed troops (Palestinian clubman, in this example) could be sent out between the ranks to attack the milling horsemen. The fact that *pilum* have still been found at military sites throughout the third century show that this new type of formation was by no means rigidly adopted.[7]

No doubt the classic legionary tactics of 'throw *pila*, then close to fight with swords' continued to be utilised where and when appropriate. Indeed, Zosimus describes how the infantry at Emesa:

> wheeled their ranks around and attacked the enemy [cavalry] as it was scattered and confused. There followed a great slaughter as they came on with the customary weapons.

Here Zosimus is referencing a style of fighting with *pilum* and sword that had remained unchanged for centuries.

In time, of course, the numbers of spearmen within a Roman legion increased as the Roman cavalry itself became the primary offensive force on the battlefield. The infantry by the fourth century may have instead acted only to block the opposing horsemen rather than defeat them – the logical end product of a military development foreshadowed by Arrian two centuries earlier. Against opposing infantry, Roman units of this later period were still formidable. Armed with a variety of ranged weapons, spears and long swords, the fourth century legion had evolved into an adaptable, mobile and aggressive combat unit.

The Bow

Bows have a long history in warfare. The Romans realised early on the value of the eastern recurve bow, a bow that was manufactured using several materials to increase its flexibility, strength and inherent power. Traditionally wood, horn and animal sinew were used, the wood made up the core of the bow with horn strips on the inner surface and sinew on the outer surface. The manufacture of these bows was a long and difficult process but the bows produced were far superior to the single-wood 'self-bows' used by the Germans, Gauls and Britons of the period. Often the ends or 'ears' of the bow were strengthened with bone 'laths' and the body of the bow was carefully covered with leather to protect it from moisture. Wet conditions could ruin a recurve bow, as could misuse. Leaving the bow stringed and ready for action ruins the springiness of these bows and reduces their power. Unlike the sling, specialist craftsmen were needed to make these complex weapons.

Arrows used by third century archers had either socketed or tanged heads and varied in their shape. Some had three blades, some two, some were used for setting fires, some were 'bodkin' types that could punch through mail armour. All were held securely in cylindrical leather quivers slung over the archer's back. Thumb-rings of bronze, bone or leather were used by archers trained in eastern units, these rings eased the pressure on the thumb which was used in the eastern archery tradition to pull back the string. An archer used to the western method of drawing employs the first two or three fingers of his right hand to draw the string. The eastern thumb-ring release is difficult to adapt to and requires a great deal of strength in the right thumb.

The range of a bow is dependent on many factors, but a skilled archer can hit a human-sized target effectively at distances of up to 80–100 m. Vegetius states that archers, like slingers, should practice their aim by shooting at a straw target 180 m distant. Greater ranges are possible of course, and when fighting as a unit that is targeting an enemy formation, precision archery is not required. Instead volleys can be shot high into the air over one's own troops to land onto the heads of the enemy force. Estimates, and practical experiments, have suggested that a skilled archer can achieve battlefield hits out to 200 or 300 m with some hope of target penetration.

The Sling

The sling was an ancient weapon that had been used by shepherds and mountain-folk for centuries. Most legionaries were given some basic training in the use of the sling because, although it was difficult to use accurately, it was cheap, portable and supplied by an unlimited source of ammunition (stones). A sling was no more than a pouch of leather connected to two leather cords at either end. Whipped over the head at great speed, a stone could be discharged with incredible force. Some slings were made of woven grass or animal hair depending on the people making them and the materials available to them. Many tribal cultures, such as the mercenary slingers from the Balearic Islands, wove their slings but a Roman legion with lots of cow hide available would find it easier to cut slings from leather. In fact a decorated leather sling pouch was found at the Vindolanda fort near Hadrian's Wall.

The author has made a replica of the Vindolanda sling and become quite proficient in its use. The pouch is around 15 cm long, and the two leather cords are 60 cm long. One cord ends in a loop and fits over the index finger, the other cord ends in a knot which is pinched between thumb and forefinger. To release the stone during a sling, the knot is released and the stone flies toward the target. Two things become immediately clear when one begins to practise with the sling; it is a deadly weapon worthy of respect, and it takes a huge amount of practise to become even moderately proficient in its use. Slinging smooth pebbles out to 70 or 80 metres becomes fairly easy fairly quickly, but hitting a human-sized target at anything beyond 30 m is difficult. For a cohort of slingers, accuracy would not have been a great concern. The objective for the unit as a whole was to cast their sling stones and simply hit the enemy formation, obviously this will be a large and relatively immobile target. Troops with minimal training would have been able to achieve this.

Difficulties arise when slinging at distance, in bad weather, or for accuracy. Contrary to a popular misconception, the sling is not whirled around the head at fantastic speed before being released. After only one or two revolutions the sling stone has already reached its maximum potential speed and further spinning just ruins the slinger's aim. Everything hangs on the timing of the release. In fact, through experimentation, the author has found that a single 'snap' motion provides a good deal of accuracy and power.

> They should also be accustomed to rotating the sling once only about the head, when the stone is discharged from it.
>
> Vegetius 1.16

The slinger can attempt one of three broad styles: overhead, over arm and under arm. Very likely the trainer passed on the slinging method that he himself had first been taught. Slingers in the Roman army would also create their own bullets (*glandes*) of lead, of baked clay or even carved stone. Using smooth beach pebbles, the author noticed that it was difficult to increase accuracy because each stone was of a slightly different shape, a different weight and often a different density. Despite a consistent and methodical slinging style, the variations in the stones created variation in accuracy. Military slingers commonly melted lead into clay or stone moulds to create a reliable and consistent form of ammunition. Practising with these *glandes* meant that a soldier could begin to improve his accuracy. Some moulds were simply sand trays with the impressions of spear butts or even thumbs in them. In addition to increased accuracy, the great density of lead meant that the sling bullets travelled faster and further and with much more power. Lead shot could easily match the range of a bow, and kill just as easily. Sling stones and bullets were invisible in flight, unlike arrows, and could not be dodged or easily defended against, in addition they were not affected by cross-winds as the fletchings on arrows were (although slinging in any kind of wind is difficult because the thongs tend to spin and tangle during reloading).

Should the effectiveness of the sling be doubted, a Persian column outside the city of Emesa in 260 was driven off solely by slingers. Led by a priest of Aphrodite, called Sampsigeramus, these 'rustic slingers', killed the Persian leader with a sling stone to the head, then the Persians 'all fled to the (frontier) with the rustic slingers and Sampsigeramus in pursuit. They vanished leaving behind the booty.'[8]

8

The Soldier's Experience

'To the spirits of the departed and in everlasting memory of Vitalinius Felix, veteran of Legio I M(inervia), a most wise and trustworthy man, seller of pottery ware at Lugdunum, who lived fifty-nine years, five months, ten days, was born on a Tuesday (the day of Mars), enlisted on a Tuesday, received his discharge on a Tuesday, and died on a Tuesday, Vitalinius Felicissimus, son, and Julia Nice, wife, had this set up and dedicated it...'

CIL 13.1906, Lugdunum (Lyon), Lugdunensis

Weaponry was an important and ever changing aspect of the Roman military system. Yet warfare was dependant, not on technology and firepower, but on the morale and muscle-power of human beings. Kingdoms were toppled, tribes enslaved and cities stormed through the adrenaline-pumped muscles of legionaries and auxiliaries who wielded swords and threw javelins.

In the story of the transformation of the Roman legions in the third century, the experience of the soldiers themselves forms a crucial element. *Spatha*, *pilum* and shields, the ironmongery of war tell part of the story – politics, strategy and the campaigns of Rome's foes tell another. At the centre of the Roman military story, though, is the day to day existence of the soldier: who he was, what he did, how he fought and what his life both inside and outside of the fort was like.

On Joining Up

When we talk of 'Roman soldiers' in the third century we are in actual fact discussing an incredibly diverse group of men, most of whom had never set foot in Rome. The popular conception is of Roman soldiers born and raised in Italy, joining the legions for service in distant wars. The author has spoken to visitors on Hadrian's Wall who felt pity for the troops ordered to garrison that remote frontier, wrenched from the sunny climes of Italy. Yet most of the troops occupying the Roman forts along the Wall were auxiliaries from other parts of northern Europe, including Dacia, Belgium and northern France, where winters could be just as harsh as those in Northumbria! Examples of some of these units include three cohorts of Pannonians and one of Dacians (all from Hungary), three cohorts of Tungrians (from Belgium) and cohorts of Morini (Normandy), Frisians (Netherlands) and Vangiones (Germany).

As discussed in Chapter 2, the Roman military system was divided into legions, manned by imperial citizens, and auxiliary cohorts, manned by non-citizen recruits from the provinces or fringes of empire, that were loyal to Rome. Two things began to change the Italian make-up of the early legions; firstly, citizenship began to be granted to some provincials as a reward, and secondly, legions could be based within a remote frontier province for generations.

In established provinces, with a growing citizenry, the legions offered many men an attractive career. If the legion remained in the province for some time it would recruit locally and there would be no shortage of veteran's sons eager to follow in their father's footsteps. Over time the manpower of the legion contained fewer and fewer Italians and increasing numbers of locals. In a study by Giovanni Forni, of 2,056 legionary dedications from the second half of the second century, only thirty-seven were of Italian descent.[1]

Auxiliary cohorts, on the other hand, were always (with one rare exception) recruited from newly conquered tribes or non-citizens within frontier provinces. That exception was *cohors* II Italica Civium Romanorum, a Roman cohort based in Palestine that was probably manned by Italian citizens.

In times of peace, potential recruits faced a *probatio*, a recruiting board, that examined the recruit physically, tested his knowledge of Latin and checked his legal status. Some recruits provided letters of recommendation in an attempt to improve their chances. Literary evidence shows that they were enlisted between the ages of 18 and 21 but studies of tombstones have revealed more than one soldier who joined up in his mid-teens. The writer Vegetius recommended that recruits be drawn from the country since:

> They are nurtured under the open sky in a life of work... and for whom wielding iron, digging a fosse and carrying a burden is what they are used to from the country.[2]

Once the young man had successfully passed the *probatio* he was termed a *tiro* (new recruit). Four months into his service with his training complete, the *tiro* swore the sacred oath, the *sacramentum*, which bound him to the legion and the service of the emperor. He received a piece of lead called the *signaculum* to mark his status and this may have been worn like a modern-day military dog tag.

A new recruit into the legions needed to be trained. As in any army, then or now, this training served two purposes, to pass on skills and abilities that would later be needed in warfare, and also (equally importantly) to indoctrinate the recruit. This military indoctrination came in the form of severe physical and mental stress designed to breakdown the soldier's identity and independence, replacing it with instinctive obedience and total loyalty to the legionary standards (the flags, images and symbols of the unit) that accompanied the troops into battle.

Recruits trained to fight with the sword by practising against a post, they were marched across country carrying heavy loads 'at the military step', taught to throw javelins and master the Roman combat drill. This was taught by drillmasters (*campidoctores*) who were officers within the infantry units. Vegetius mentions another training officer, the *doctores armorum* or weapons instructor, and he tells us that these men were rewarded with double pay due to their status and importance. Soldiers failing to meet either the standards of drill or weapon proficiency had their wheat rations downgraded to barley (which was something shameful, ordinarily barley was reserved for the cavalry horses and not eaten by the soldiers).

Not all training took place in and around the fort. Skills such as the marching, camp construction, and river crossing could only be learnt in the countryside. Several times each month a garrison, both infantry and cavalry together, had to engage in 'manoeuvres' (*ambulatum*). These exercises resembled war-games, with units deploying, marching and camping overnight in order to hone their skills. Vegetius quotes from the constitutions of Augustus and Hadrian and states that *ambulatum* occurred three times a month, other documents argue that it was carried out either every seven or every five days.

At the Fort

When archaeologists begin to dig a new Roman fort, they are reasonably sure of what buildings they will find, know something of the building's dimensions and some idea of their approximate location. Although Roman forts are certainly not identical (there being a number of aberrant designs) they are usually very similar and this generally holds true across the empire. Most troops were garrisoned either in large legionary fortresses or in much smaller forts. The distinction between fortress and fort is a modern one based on the supposed troop garrison it supported. Fortresses are associated with legions while forts are associated with auxiliary cohorts or cavalry units.

This separation of use was once thought to be clear cut but it seems more likely that legions and auxiliaries could often be mixed together. The fortresses were large, with capacity enough to house an entire legion of around 5,000 men (some like Xanten, on the Rhine, could house two full legions). Auxiliary forts on the other hand were built to house a cohort of either 500 or 1,000 men. Finds of military equipment suggest that small numbers of legionaries were sometimes based at auxiliary forts, and in a similar vein there may on occasion have been auxiliaries living and working within some of the legionary fortresses. Sites like

Longthorpe in England, which have produced *pila*, javelins and *lorica segmentata* seem to be vexillation forts, housing units of legionaries and auxiliaries together.[3]

A fortress like Caerleon (Isca Silurum) in South Wales was laid out in a standard 'playing card' shape, a rectangle around 500 m long and 400 m wide with rounded corners. Defences consisted of multiple deep ditches and a high stone wall backed by a turf rampart, the ditches had a V-shaped section, which would have made it difficult for an enemy force to cross. The stone wall of the fortress was broken by double-span gates, each one set into one of the four sides. Although it is difficult to calculate, the walls may have had a walkway for the use of troops on guard-duty, and they may have been a little over 4 m high. Each gateway was fortified with two imposing towers and towers also stood at each corner of the fort and at intervals along the inner wall.

Buildings within the fortress were laid out to a regular street plan. There were two roads in particular that formed the focus of the plan, the *via principalis* which connected the gateways on the long walls, and the *via praetoria* which led from the main gate (*porta praetoria*) to the headquarters building which lay on the other side of the *via principalis*. A third road connected the gateway called the *porta decumana* to the central range of buildings. Other buildings and roads fitted into this basic layout. There were granaries, barracks, workshops, stables, a hospital, a grand house for the commanding officer and lesser houses for his tribunes, a bath-house and various minor buildings perhaps including latrines, workshops, armouries and store sheds.

The barrack blocks that housed the legionaries played a fundamental part in their lives. Each block was built to house around 80 men and consisted of a long, narrow range of rooms that ended in a suite of rooms for the centurion commanding those men. This arrangement mimicked the layout of the legion's tents whilst on campaign. The *contubernium* ('tent party') would erect its tent in line with all the others of the unit and the centurion had his tent pitched at the end of that line. In this way a Roman marching camp was well organised. Inside the fort the same arrangement was followed, except that instead of a tent the squad was allocated a pair of rooms, one behind the other and linked by a doorway.

Part of the fort's headquarters building seems to have often served as a central weapons store (*armamentarium*) with its own officer (*custodes armorum*) but these armouries are unlikely to have held all of a soldier's equipment, concentrating instead on collective kit and on armour and weapon repairs. In some cases helmets and even spears have been inscribed by the owner to indicate personal possession. Was this kit hung from pegs? Stacked on shelves? Placed in chests or pushed under the beds? In all probability all of these. It seems likely that a *contubernium* prepared its own food and ate together, either sat on stools or on their bunks, or outside under the colonnade.

The centurion would have had his quarters in the spacious rooms at the end of the block, not just sleeping and living accommodation but also offices, a lavatory and rooms for servants and family. These apartments would have been nicely furnished, and decorated with wall-paintings.

Commanding officers, tribunes and legionary legates did not live 'in barracks'. The commander resided in a splendid Roman house that sat adjacent to the headquarters' building, close to the centre of the fort. In the huge legionary fortresses, such as the Legio VI's base at Eboracum, this commander's house (*praetorium*) was itself a magnificent palace, with courtyards, dining rooms, mosaic-floored corridors and a multitude of rooms. Of course the tribune commanding a small auxiliary force on the very edge of empire did not have a palace but he certainly had one of the most lavishly decorated and well-appointed houses in the area. This was a Roman house for a man of rank.

The nerve-centre of every fort in the Roman military system was the headquarters building (*principia*). It lay at the very centre of the fortress or auxiliary fort and was the fort's office, its command centre and strong-room. Since it was the first stop for any visitor to the fort the entrance to the principia was architecturally impressive. This entrance opened out into a high-walled colonnaded courtyard paved with flagstones. A well was often located in a corner of the courtyard and there is some evidence (such as at Housesteads and Künzing) that the rooms arranged around this courtyard stored weaponry, equipment and armour. In the far wall opposite the gateway was a doorway into a large cross hall. The hall, or basilica, was the beating heart of every fort. This lofty hall had rows of columns running down its length. It may be that the hall served as an assembly point for the unit. A tribunal, or raised stone platform, sat at one end that enabled the commanding officer to review small units of troops or to provide briefings to officers. Here the commander could dispense justice, issue important orders and present awards to heroic individuals.

Directly across the middle of the hall stood the doorway into the shrine of the standards (*sacellum*), either side of which was a suite of offices. One set of offices was used by the military clerks who were led by an officer called the *cornicularius*. A huge amount of paperwork would have been processed by these men, logging everything from sick-leave to hobnail pay-outs, the height of new recruits to daily duty rosters. The other set of offices was traditionally used by the regimental standard bearers (*signiferi*) who were responsible not only for the military standards of the entire legion but also for the pay and the savings of the troops. The shrine itself housed the standards of the unit; beneath it a stone-lined cellar held the unit's pay chests.

Every fort had granaries (*horrea*) but they were in reality general storehouses since they held all manner of foodstuffs, and were not merely barns filled with sacks of grain. Each granary was massively built with buttresses that helped support a wide roof designed to keep rainwater well away from the immediate vicinity of the building. Damp would quickly spoil any dry food held in storage. In order to further reduce the effects of damp, granaries were raised up on pillars, allowing air to circulate.

Every Roman fort had a number of long buildings with an indeterminate use. It is likely (on the evidence of finds) that these buildings were workshops (*fabricae*), providing the troops with the material support they needed to operate. All manner of craft activities would be practised here, from carpentry to metalwork, boot-manufacture to leatherwork. While large scale production was carried out by civilian contractors, the fortress workshops probably produced minor goods and repaired damaged military equipment.

An extraordinary feature of the huge legionary fortresses across the empire was the existence of a military hospital (*valetudinarium*), usually sited close to the centre of the military enclosure. In only a few instances so far have hospitals been positively identified in the smaller auxiliary forts. This building and its trained staff gave wounded troops a much improved chance of survival. It also served to provide care for those soldiers suffering illness or disease, or those unfortunates who were recovering from surgery. Roman medicine was extremely advanced in comparison to many contemporary cultures and surgery was certainly performed at these hospitals. Depending on the size of the fort or the medical demands placed on it, the *valetudinarium* could either take the form of a courtyard building, or of a barrack block. In the latter case, the hospital might have one large ward, or be divided up into smaller rooms that could accommodate half a dozen patients at one time.

Lesser buildings would certainly exist alongside these more important structures. Wells, water tanks and communal latrines were very necessary amenities that no fort could do without. There might also be a series of bread ovens built into the earthen rampart on the inner face of the fortress wall. These ovens would be used on some sort of rota basis by the different units in the fort. The separate *contubernia* usually received grain rations, not baked bread, and they would have had to grind the grain, make the dough and have it baked at the fort's ovens before it could be turned into a meal. Military bread stamps have been discovered, evidence that bread was probably marked by the century that it was being baked for.

Life in Peacetime

Soldiers identified with the eight-man *contubernium* or tent-party that they belonged to, sharing meals and rooms with these men and probably fighting in the battle-line alongside them. At the fort there would be guard duty, maintenance, local patrols and training to fill the soldier's time. Those who were promoted to *immunis* were able to take up a trade that exempted them from the more onerous tasks, others who were able to read and write might be able to gain a promotion into the administrative staff of the *cornicularis*.

Fragments of duty rosters have survived from first century Egypt as well as Vindolanda, on Hadrian's Wall. They show a remarkably diverse number of duties, jobs and assignments, everything from road patrol, drainage, workshop duty, latrine cleaning, gate guard, armoury or bath-house duty, centurion's assistant and even assignment to some distant city (or even province). Some centurions were amenable to bribes in order to dish out the most favourable duties.

Centurions were well known for dishing out punishments, too. The strength of the Roman army came from its regime of continual training, coupled with incredibly high standards of discipline. Beatings and floggings were common punishments for lesser offences, whilst the most serious, which included sleeping while on guard duty or running away during battle, were punishable by execution. For the sleepy sentry the execution came in the form of being stoned to death by one's own comrades, vividly illustrating that it was their safety the accused was putting in danger.

With the prospect of death, injury or maiming on the battlefield and the harsh discipline inside the Roman fortress one wonders why recruits were so eager to join the legions. It certainly was not for the pay; both Septimius Severus and Caracalla had increased the meagre allowance but nevertheless it did not constitute a fortune. Severus increased legionary pay to around 450 denarii a year, paid in three instalments on 1 January, 1 May and 1 September. The amount received was considerably less after stoppages. Deductions were made for clothing, food, boots, equipment, the burial club and even the yearly Saturnalia festival. Instead a soldier's main monetary income came from donatives, gifts of silver and gold paid to the legions by the emperor. These appeals for loyalty

Tombstone of M.Aurelius Lucianus, Rome.
(*after Bishop and Coulston*)

celebrated the emperor's birthday and his accession to the throne (though this latter was paid every five years).

Income could also be supplemented by acts of bravery and donatives could be awarded to men in battle who distinguished themselves. This incentive certainly urged men forward to take risks, some were reckless enough to take off their helmets as they fought in order to be noticed by their commanders. Titus, commander of the Roman forces besieging Jerusalem in 70, offered to promote any soldier who would lead the suicidal attack over the collapsed wall of the fortress Antonia. One man named Sabinus stepped forward:

> yet anyone who had seen him before would have concluded ... that he was not even an average soldier ... his flesh lean and shrunken; but in his frail body, far too slender for its own prowess, dwelt a heroic soul. Sabinus led eleven other men over the wall, but he, along with three others, were killed and never received their promotions.

The achievements of a senior centurion named Titus Aurelius Flavinus who fought in Caracalla's German campaign, were recorded on an honorary inscription found in Moesia. It declared that he was:

> honoured by the Divine Great Antoninus Augustus with 50,000 sesterces and 25,000 sesterces and promotion on account of his dashing bravery against the (German) forces ...[4]

Promotion allowed a recruit to change his social status. Learning a trade elevated him above the mass of the *milites* (common soldiers) and promotion to the rank of *principalis* (junior officer) which pushed up pay and enhanced prospects further. It was even possible for a soldier, working through the ranks, to gain entry into the centurianate. Far more than simply junior officers, these officers were the bones of a legion carrying with them the experience and traditions of the unit. Socially they were far removed from the *milites*, enjoying a suite of rooms, servants, high status and an annual *stipendium*, following Caracalla's increases, in excess of 12,000 denarii. Most centurions seem to have had origins amongst the wealthy equestrian classes of Rome, entering the legion at a relatively young age.

What did the soldier spend his money on? Amongst other things, gambling, which was popular in the legionary bath-house and the taverns and inns of the local civilian settlement. This unplanned town or village typically grew up right outside the fortress walls and accommodated traders and craftsmen eager to cater to the off-duty soldier. Here too were the wine shops and inns, stables, temples, brothels, workshops and food stalls. Often very large towns would develop outside of legionary fortresses, whilst smaller villages (known as *vici*) thrived outside the smaller forts. If a soldier had a girlfriend, a wife or a family, then they would probably be living within the nearby civilian settlement. The population of these *vici* was very cosmopolitan. Slaves, traders and veteran soldiers from all across the empire rubbed shoulders with provincial locals quick to see a profit in this captive market of men with nowhere else to spend their wages.

Prior to the reign of Severus, soldiers had been forbidden to marry and were even forced to divorce upon joining the legion. This did not prevent long-term relationships with local women, however, or with former slaves who were freed by their soldier-owners. Few of these women were Roman citizens and so sons and daughters did not automatically gain their father's citizenship status. To curry favour with his legions, Severus over-turned the two-hundred-year-old law. This not only legitimised on-going relationships but provided both wife and off-spring with Roman citizenship. During the third century the sons of legionaries, born in the shadow of the fortress walls, could now join up and follow their fathers into the ranks. It might be hard to believe that soldiers had the freedom to visit families outside the fortress and to sleep outside of the barrack block and raise a family but some research goes even further and suggests that women and children may actually have been allowed to live with the troops inside their barrack blocks. Crowded this may have been but families in Rome were already sharing similarly cramped spaces in tenement blocks. Add to this the small army of slaves that soldiers kept as personal servants (*galearii*) and we have a picture of a rambunctious and crowded military fortress, half township-half military camp. [5]

Much of what we know about third century soldiers comes from tombstones such as those found at Apamea. Since the dead were not allowed to be buried inside a settlement, a local cemetery typically sat on one or more of the main roads that led away from the fortress and its *vicus*. Inscriptions often name the patron of a tombstone and this is typically a wife, a son, or other relative.

Most *vici* could offer at least one small temple for the use of soldiers and locals alike. Often they would be devoted to a classical Roman deity or more likely to a local provincial deity that could be equated with someone like Mars or Artemis or Apollo. Romans were open to the gods of foreign lands, worshipping them just as fervently as those of the classical pantheon. The city of Dura Europus, located on the dangerous Syrian frontier facing the Persian kingdom, could boast twenty four temples. Temples to classical deities such as Artemis, Zeus and Jupiter existed, though these gods were also associated with a local deity; more exotic Syrian gods, like Aphlad, Atargatis, Bel and Azzanathkona had their own temples. Soldiers offered sacrifices to all of these according to their preferences or their needs. On other frontiers local gods were venerated including Gebrinius and Loucetios along the Rhine frontier and Cocidius and Coventina in Britain.

Superstition and religion were intertwined and magical symbols were popular amongst soldiers. Phallic charms (*fascina*) could be worn as an amulet to ward off evil, with some soldiers favouring a version known as the 'fist and phallus' a double-ended design found across the empire. Other symbols with supernatural meaning included the swastika (known to the Romans as a *crux gammatica*), which on the Indian subcontinent today represents good fortune. Brooch finds in the form of a swastika are quite widespread across the Roman world from Britain to Syria, generally they date to the later second century and into the third. Tunics could also be decorated with the swastika motif, examples from the fourth century are found on the Piazza Armerina mosaic from Sicily as well as the Via Latina catacomb paintings in Rome.

The legion itself constituted a religious body and the standards carried by the *signiferi* (the standard bearers) were venerated by the troops. These standards included the eagle, proud emblem of a legion, an image of the emperor, the emblem or animal totem of the legion, the *vexillum* or flag bearing the name and titles of the unit, as well as others. These standards were carried on poles by junior officers and were locked in the shrine of the standards (*sacellum*) at the heart of the headquarters building, brought out for all official occasions. Roman soldiers were led in the communal worship of Jupiter, Minerva and Mars as well as any other gods favoured by the unit. There is no mention of priests living amongst the soldiers but a wall painting from the Temple of Bel at Dura Europus (dated to the mid-third century) actually shows the garrison commander, tribune Julius Terentius, sacrificing before three statues. His men are lined up behind him, with right hands raised in prayer. Facing the tribune is the unit's standard bearer, holding the *vexillum* for all the troops to see. The commander would officiate over ceremonies held (most likely) on the parade ground or before battle, ceremonies which including animal sacrifice and the reading and interpretation of omens. The imperial cult and the cult of Rome formed the basis for collective religious worship within the unit.

One eastern cult had gained ground rapidly within the legions of the third century. Although congregations were small judging by the size of temple floor plans, the cult of Mithras enjoyed great status. Worshippers met in small, cave-like temples called *mithraea* which have been found in Germany, Italy, Hungary, France, Syria (including an example at Dura Europus), Britain and elsewhere.

The cult was popular amongst soldiers, it was tough and masculine and fostered a brotherly comradeship with a male-only community that helped fellow initiates to face dark times with bravery and stoicism. There was no place for women in this religion, and indeed the worshippers had to be initiated with a rather unpleasant series of rituals before being allowed to join the first rank of members (the Ravens). Further initiations were possible that could see an experienced cult member rise through the grades, as Bridegroom, Soldier, Lion, Persian, Heliodromos and finally Father. This was a sun cult with aspects of magic and astrology that had its origins in the Persian east. Mithras was a sun hero, a champion of the world who slew the Sacred Bull and fought against demons to bring life to the universe.

Bust of the god Mithras, from the Walbrook Mithraeum in London.

The *mithraea* were always small, typically holding a congregation of around twenty people, yet there must have been many more followers of Mithras in the typical garrison. The cult was extremely popular amongst the army and actually carried from one province to another when units received new postings. Perhaps the worship of Mithras at the stone-built temples outside Roman forts was quite exclusive, limited only to the officers of the fort. With officers gathered together, sharing ideas and drink, breaking bread and swearing secret oaths of brotherly loyalty, the *mithraea* might have resembled elite officers' clubs. Elsewhere, in towns and ports, the cult was not elitist; poor men, freedmen, senators and hard-working Roman tradesmen could all be initiated, although one suspects that membership was by invitation only.

On the March

The Roman roads that criss-crossed the empire were built to facilitate the movement of troops from one garrison to another or to reach a trouble-spot in time to bolster the local defences. Soldiers were accustomed to marching long distances. Every soldier, then as now, was familiar with life on the march. His unit may be transferring to a new location, lock-stock-and-barrel, or it may be moving quickly, without baggage and pack animals, to deal with a barbarian incursion or uprising. These marches would generally be made on the Roman roads constructed for that very purpose, but once in the area of enemy activity, cross-country marches away from well-surfaced roads would be undertaken.

The writer Vegetius tells us that recruits were trained to march 20 Roman miles (30 km) in five hours at a 'military step', and 24 Roman miles (35 km) in five hours at the 'full step'. This kind of speed was designed to get a legion or a *vexillation* to its destination without becoming strung out or disordered on the march. On campaign the soldiers would habitually travel at the much reduced speed of the baggage animals. Away from the Roman road network, marching across country, the speed of a unit would have been reduced even further. The experiences of modern soldiers bear out Vegetius' numbers, it seems that 32 km (20 miles) is a good day's walk for a loaded infantryman.

The fighting load consisted of the armour, helmet, large round or oval shield and all the weaponry that the infantryman needed to participate in a full-scale battle. Typically as much armour as possible was worn, particularly by the file-leaders who fought at the front. This panoply was heavy; the author's reconstructed shield weighs around 8 kg, his suit of ringmail (short-sleeved and thigh-length) weighs 14 kg. Add to this iron leg protection (*greaves*), a padded *subarmalis*, military belt, a *spatha*, a *pilum* and helmet and his reconstructed fighting load weighs in at a total of 30 kg.

Marching rations needed to be light in weight and preserved for later consumption, often by drying or smoking. These rations were designed to last for many days in the field. Ammianus relates how the fourth century Emperor Julian rebuilt forts along the River Meuse during his campaigns against the German tribes and provisioned them by taking part of the seventeen days' rations which the troops carried on their backs. We have other sources which tell us how bleak the marching diet was. Vegetius remarks that soldiers should have 'grain (i.e. wheat), wine, vinegar and salt at all times'. That wheat ration will have come as hardtack biscuits. The emperor Hadrian lived the life of a regular soldier for a while and enjoyed '*larido, caseo et posca*', which was bacon fat, cheese and sour wine (also called *acetum*). Remember that hardtack was a way to preserve the wheat ration; it was essential. Soldiers may even have ground it down in their mixing bowls (*mortaria*) to turn it back into flour with which they could bake fresh bread. Grains of wheat or barley could also be carried but they would need to be ground up using a portable millstone carried by the *contubernium's* mule.

The mule also carried the large squad tent made of goatskin panels stitched together, as well as a number of construction tools. Legionaries were engineers as well as warriors and took all manner of construction and excavation tools with them on campaign. With these they built their marching camps as well as anything else their commanders required, from a palisade fence to a watch-tower, from a wooden bridge to a permanent frontier fort.

In the first century, the legionary carried with him his arms and armour, as well as other essential equipment that included 'saw and basket, axe and pick, a strap, reaping hook, chain and three days' rations, so that there is not much difference between a foot-soldier and a pack-mule!' Both hand-saw and axe were useful in cutting timbers ready for fort or palisade construction, while the pick and basket were used to shift earth and dig out the defensive ditches. The strap of leather or rope may have been used to carry turves on the shoulder, as legionaries are shown doing on Trajan's Column.[6]

We know from military handbooks and excavated finds that the legions of the third and fourth century relied on exactly the same pieces of equipment as their first century predecessors. A squad had its own pick-axes (*dolabra*), hand-axes, an adze, a saw, a mattock (*ligo*) or two, a hammer, a couple of shovels, a basket, sickles (*falces*) and some coarse cloth (perhaps for making sacks). These tools were shared amongst the squad, just as the work was to be shared. When it came time to construct the marching camp, some members of the *contubernium* could help fell trees, while others might be lifting turves, digging the perimeter ditch or sawing timber to create new palisade stakes. All could work simultaneously with the tools they had at their disposal.

Vegetius described the ideal formation for a column marching to war. At the head is placed the bulk of the cavalry and behind it the infantry. In the centre of the column is placed all of the baggage, the wagons, pack animals and the servants. Finally the rear-guard should be composed of light cavalry and skirmish troops. Additional light or heavy troops could be deployed to screen the baggage portion of the column, and protect the vulnerable flanks. When a commander suspected (perhaps via information provided by scouting patrols) that an enemy force might try to ambush the column, he might reinforce one part of the column or another with additional troops. These troops, Vegetius tells us, are best employed as a reaction force, able to quickly move to intercept an enemy ambush or pursue fleeing attackers. Consequently, picked cavalry, light infantry and archers were preferred for this type of duty.

Both Vegetius and Maurice warn of the panic and potentially deadly confusion that arises when a column on the march comes under attack, and both provide a measure of advice to mitigate that confusion. Marching with hundreds of other soldiers, overburdened with equipment and supplies, trying to keep in formation, trying to keep one's footing and not slip or trip, it is not surprising that legionaries would not expect, nor be easily able to react to, a sudden attack. The author has discovered from past experience that unless one carries a shield in the hand and does not sling it on one's back, it is difficult to bring it around ready for instant use. Indeed one of the strongest pieces of advice given by the ancient writers was that troops should carry their shields and spears in their hands (rather than packing them in the wagons, one suspects).

9

The Persian Onslaught

'As for you wretched Syria, I weep for you with great pity. To you too will come a fearful attack by bow-shooting men, which you never expected to befall you. The fugitive of Rome will come, brandishing a great spear, crossing the Euphrates with many thousands, who will put you to the torch and maltreat everything.... Having despoiled you and stripped you of everything, he will leave you roofless and uninhabited. Suddenly anyone who sees you will weep for you.'

The Thirteenth Sibylline Oracle (c. AD 253)

In 253 Roman forces had marched against one another in order to defend their choice of emperor. Valerian and his son, Gallienus, had been the victors in that relatively bloodless showdown, north of Rome. Bloodless it may have been, but Valerian had marched into Italy at the head of an army that he had been ordered to raise for a campaign on the upper Danube. Valerian had been given that job by emperor Trebonianus Gallus and once news of Gallus' assassination reached Valerian, he had decided to move the Danube legions into Italy – he planned to take the throne away from the usurper, Aemilianus.

This crisis of succession and of legitimacy in 253 obscured the real danger. Not only had the Danube frontier been weakened by the removal of its troops to support Valerian's claim on Rome, but in the east the ruin and destruction wrought by the energetic Shapur, ruler of Sassanid Persia, still smouldered.

Shapur Takes the East

> The wicked Shapur of whom I have spoken succeeded him (Ardashir) and lived on for thirty-one years more, doing great harm to the Romans
>
> Agathias 4.24

Valerian was not a young man, he was already fifty-eight when he took the throne and his son, Gallienus, was forty. In a way this provided the new emperor with a nominated successor and a loyal co-emperor from day one of his reign. This situation might have been able to provide the stability that the empire desperately needed, but Fate would cruelly intervene. Leaving his son to organise the defence of the west, the emperor set out immediately for Syria in order to restore the situation there. He would never return.

Antioch was the second city of the Roman Empire and the shock of its fall and destruction resonates in the writings from the time. Although Roman forces had been soundly beaten at the battle of Barbalissos in 252 and much of Syria then occupied and plundered by Persian raiding forces, it seems that its jewel, Antioch, fell to King Shapur a year later. The city was offered to the Persians by the traitor, Myriades. This man had been a wealthy senator who had been expelled from the city for embezzling funds that were destined for the chariot races. In revenge Myriades offered his services to Shapur and led the troops directly to the gates. The rich fled from Antioch at the approach of the Persians, leaving behind the restless masses who seemed to be quite content with a change of government.

Shapur had ordered a huge battering ram to be fashioned, its head was indeed in the shape of a ram and solidly made of iron. It was massive, and once it had served its purpose was dragged to the city of Carrhae and abandoned. A hundred years later this same 'antique' ram would be dragged to the city of Bezabde by the legions in order to dislodge the Persians from that city. The fall of Antioch must have been sudden and unexpected, Eunapius writes how a comic actor on stage within the city suddenly declared to his audience, 'Am I dreaming or are the Persians here?' His audience fled in terror as missiles rained down upon them, the houses and temples were plundered, inhabitants killed or taken into captivity and the city set on fire. The treacherous Myriades, history records, was executed by Shapur once the city had been captured.[1]

Valerian mustered his Roman forces and fought the Persian garrisons left behind by Shapur. It must have seemed to the emperor that he was making light work of the Persian occupation and raiding troops, but the King of Kings was holding his elite cavalry forces in reserve further east. An unnamed Roman victory in 257 was even substantial enough to be commemorated on an issue of coins bearing Valerian's name.

When Valerian discovered that Shapur was besieging Edessa with great difficulty in 260, he launched a military expedition to fight the Persians there. However, the plains around Edessa and Carrhae were much suited to Persian cavalry and in addition the Roman troops were far outnumbered. Not only that but the *equites* Mauri (the Moorish cavalry) were stricken with the plague. Suffering a terrible defeat in June of that year and forced to retreat behind the walls of Edessa, Valerian had run out of options. Persian inscriptions claim that the Roman force had numbered 70,000 and that a great number were captured and deported to Iran. The emperor decided to attempt negotiation, it was perhaps the only option left to him. Shapur insisted he leave Edessa to talk, accompanied only by a small retinue of advisors and officers. Upon receiving the Roman delegation, the 'wicked and bloodthirsty' king captured them all. Valerian, the emperor of Rome, as well as high ranking Roman senators, the praetorian prefect and many others, were all enslaved. No emperor had ever been captured by the enemy before; the news stunned Rome.[2]

Free now to roam at will, Shapur attacked Syrian cities in a renewed military campaign, sacking Seleucia, Iconium, Nicopolis, Tyana and, once again, Antioch. The Persian army even reached Cappadocia. The Roman forces, smashed outside Edessa, were little match for the Persian army. There was some spirited resistance in Cilicia where a Roman general named Ballista rallied Roman stragglers and made attacks on the Persians, now divided into smaller, more mobile raiding parties. He was able to capture the harem of Shapur along with a great deal of booty and his troops were able to wipe out a force of three thousand Persians.

Shapur, realising he had outstayed his welcome, turned his forces east and headed for home. He first had to bribe the fierce citizens of Edessa in order that he might pass unmolested. Odaenathus, king of Palmyra, a wealthy caravan city allied with Rome, could not be bribed – and he harried the retreating Persians along the Euphrates river frontier. Thousands of prisoners were marched east by the Persians, fed on the bare minimum to support life and allowed to drink once a day, being driven to water by their guards like cattle. According to the writer Zonaras, at one point the retreating column reached a gorge impassable to Shapur's baggage animals. The king 'ordered the prisoners to be killed and thrown into the gorge so that when its depth was filled up with the bodies of the corpses, his baggage animals might make their way across.'[3]

Of course Valerian was now also a prisoner. Accounts differ about how long he survived; Aurelius Victor claims that he was quickly hacked to death, but others insist the emperor lived out his life in servitude to Shapur. *See* Colour Plate 28. As a common slave, Valerian, a man in his sixties, was humiliated and forced to stoop and allow Shapur to step on his back to mount his horse. Lactantius claims that when Valerian eventually died, the Persian king had his body skinned. The old man's skin was dyed with vermillion and then stretched upon a wall so that future ambassadors from Rome might look upon poor Valerian evermore as a symbol of Rome's military vulnerability.[4]

Had Valerian left no heir it is likely that a new round of civil wars would have torn through the empire. However, Valerian had entrusted the western half of the empire to Gallienus, his capable son and co-emperor. But if Romans had thought that the future could not get any worse, they were sorely mistaken.

The Era of Pretenders

> Now let us pass on to the twenty pretenders, who arose in the time of Gallienus because of contempt for the evil prince.
>
> Historian Augusta, Life of Gallienus 21

While Valerian spent his final years of freedom in the east waging war against the Persian army, his son Gallienus was no less busy on the northern frontier. German tribes beyond the Danube river were beaten back during the years 254 to 256, and once that frontier was secure, the focus shifted to the defence of the Rhine. Attacks came thick and fast. Although Gallienus claimed the title of 'Germanicus Maximus' for himself five times and issued coins celebrating his victories beyond the Rhine, he was soon back on the Danube (258). Yet, despite his furious fire-fighting Gallienus could not be everywhere at once and further west the Juthungi broke through the military frontier (*limes*).

From the North Sea, the river Rhine snaked southwards to provide a natural barrier against the German tribes to the east. Meanwhile, Italy, Pannonia and Thrace received the protection of the river Danube which ran from southern Germany eastwards to the Black Sea. North of this frontier, German and Sarmatian tribes squared off against the local Roman garrisons. However, these 'wet' frontiers, formidable natural moats that took great effort to breach, did not meet. This vulnerable gap at the headwaters of the Danube and the Rhine was kept free of German invaders with only a man-made defensive line. The modern-day German state of Baden-Württemberg represents the vulnerable provincial settlement known as the Agri Decumates that lay behind this frontier.

For the previous twenty years attacks had been frequent and punishing on this defensive weak point. At Castra Vetoniana (modern Pfünz) excavations seem to suggest that the soldiers of *cohors* I Breucorum had been so surprised in one attack that gate guards had no time to grab their shields. Repeated Germanic attacks eroded the military installations and their garrisons to a point that made the 259 invasion possible. The Juthungi descended on Italy and marched toward Rome where a hastily assembled army turned them back – they were defeated near Mediolanum (Milan) by the forces of Gallienus. The weakened sector of the frontier had exposed Italy to the ferocity of the northern tribes. Rome, a city without fortifications, had not felt this vulnerable since the first century BC.

Unsurprisingly, the Agri Decumates was hastily abandoned – that frontier was now considered untenable. Yet attacks continued relentlessly. The Alemanni invaded Italy in 260 while other raiders ravaged as far as Gaul and Spain. The northern borders were crumbling, as was confidence in the emperor Gallienus. Beleaguered provincials who were threatened with continued barbarian attacks, and some of the emperor's own generals, had lost faith in Gallienus' ability to defend the empire.

The Usurpers

The invasion of northern Italy and the abandonment of the Agri Decumates region, coupled with the Roman defeat at Edessa and capture of Valerian, triggered a wave of usurpers all eager to prove that they could do better. Although the Historia Augusta talks of twenty pretenders, there were in fact fewer serious contenders. First was Ingenuus, governor of Pannonia and Moesia, with plenty of legions at his command. He was defeated in battle at Mursa, northwest of modern Belgrade, by a Roman army led by one of Gallienus' top generals called Aureolus. This seething frontier produced another discontented general, Regalianus, who was proclaimed emperor by the remnants of Ingenuus' broken army in late 260. He was murdered by his own troops.

Syria had more right than most to be discontented and late in 260 the legions there threw their support behind Macrianus and Ballista, the two generals who had pulled together some kind of military response to the terrible Persian onslaught following Valerian's capture. Macrianus was hailed as emperor by the eastern troops he commanded but being of advanced age and infirm, he passed that title to his two sons, known together as the Macriani. The two brothers were named Fulvius Iunius Macrianus and Fulvius Iunius Quietus. Proclaimed joint emperors and enjoying the support of the war-weary eastern provinces they planned to take control of the empire. Macrianus (the older of the two brothers) marched against Gallienus with an army numbering 45,000. Again the general Aureolus counter-attacked and in 261 his forces encircled the army of the rebels in Illyricum (the region of former Yugoslavia). The trapped legionaries suddenly switched sides and ended the rebellion.

Quietus, the younger of the Macriani, had remained in Syria with Ballista and both men had taken refuge within the city of Edessa. Here, Gallienus was able to call on Odaenathus, an ally in the east on whom he could depend. As the ruler of wealthy Palmyra, untouched by Persian aggression, Odaenathus commanded the premier fighting force on the eastern frontier. Following the earlier Palmyrene attacks on the Persian columns and the capture of Shapur's harem, Gallienus had rewarded Odaenathus with the honorary title of *dux Romanorum* ('regional commander'). Edessa was soon besieged by the Palmyrene prince who executed Quietus and Ballista once the city had fallen. He did this on behalf of Gallienus.

The eastern uprising had been quashed but plenty of bitterness and resentment circulated throughout the empire. Mussius Aemilianus was governor of Egypt and had been part of the Macriani revolt. Now *he* claimed the throne but like the Macriani, he was defeated in battle and executed early in 262.

Even Aureolus, the emperor's trusted general, rebelled in 262 but he was forced to back down and make peace with his master. Unusually, the emperor let him retain not only his life but also his position and power. Perhaps he needed the military talent of Aureolus too much to have him executed.

Fragments of Empire

Upon the news of Valerian's capture and enslavement, the governor of Lower Germany, Marcus Cassianus Latinus Postumus, rose in revolt against Gallienus. Postumus had ably dealt with a Germanic attack and on the strength of this victory, had his troops proclaim him emperor. In the autumn of 260 he marched to Colonia Agrippina (modern Cologne) where the young son of Gallienus, Salonius, had been installed as co-emperor with his father. Postumus refused to give up the siege of the city unless Salonius was handed over to him. Once the folk of Colonia Agrippina agreed to the demands, both the boy and his guardian were executed.

Unlike past usurpers who had usually gathered together a military force and then made a dash to Rome, Postumus seemed content to remain beyond the Alps. Using the Rhine legions, he was able to clear the western provinces of barbarians and in doing so he earned the loyalty of the British, Spanish and Gallic provinces. The governors and legionary commanders decided to recognise Postumus as the legitimate emperor over those territories. This was not a re-run of power-sharing between Clodius Albinus and Septimius Severus in 193, Postumus had, in a stroke, created an alternative Roman Empire, one based primarily upon the defence of the western provinces that was ruled from Augusta Treverorum (modern Trier). Postumus made it clear that he was satisfied with the western provinces and did not spoil for a fight, this was just as well, for Gallienus was struggling to cope with a series of usurpers from 260 to 262.

It was not until the spring of 265 that Gallienus felt confident enough to challenge Postumus and marched a Roman army deep into Gaul. An early victory led to the bottling up of Postumus within a city (possibly Lugdunum, modern Lyons) followed by a siege. While the emperor inspected the siege works constructed by his troops, a defender shot Gallienus in the back with an arrow, seriously wounding him. He was evacuated back to Rome in order to recover and although Aureolus was left in charge of the conflict he seems to have made some kind of deal with Postumus, lifting the siege and letting the usurper escape. The Gallic Empire was thereafter left unmolested by Gallienus who continued to face the inevitable distractions - the renewed invasions that would continue to batter what was left of the Roman Empire.

This break-away Gallic Empire survived as an independent state for the next fourteen years; it was made up of the three provinces of Gaul (Aquitania, Narbonensis and Lugdunensis), the two German provinces (Upper and Lower), the three Spanish provinces (Tarraconensis, Lusitania and Baetica), Raetia and the two British provinces (Superior and Inferior). Raetia was taken back by Gallienus in 263 and the Spanish provinces, along with eastern Narbonensis (that area east of the Rhône) were all recovered in 269. However, a measure of the Gallic Empire's success can be gleaned not just from its relative longevity but also from the fact that all of its four emperors refused to march on Rome and they instead focused on protecting the territory from incursions beyond the Rhine. The third century 'disease', that of imperial succession by military assassination plagued the successors of Postumus just as it did Rome; all but the last of the Gallic emperors were murdered.

In a sense, the Gallic Empire depicts the Roman Empire cracking and disintegrating under pressure, and as events in Syria would soon show, it was not just the west that wanted to go its own way. The mass eastern support of the Macriani in 260 indicated a similar provincial sentiment – that of a desire for firm local control in the face of a foreign onslaught. In 270 the east would officially break away from Rome which effectively created three separate imperial powers.

In 266, as the emperor Gallienus recovered from his arrow wound, Odaenathus, the ruler of Palmyra, spearheaded his own military campaign against Persia. Driving deep into Mesopotamia he was able to win a stunning victory at Ctesiphon, the Persian capital, an achievement matched only by three Roman emperors before him. These men had the weight of Rome's military behind them; Odaenathus had his elite Palmyrene cavalry backed by the military forces of the eastern provinces. It was clear that this potentate was running the show in Syria and Mesopotamia.

From the viewpoint of Gallienus, looking outwards from Rome, the Gallic Empire in the west was dealing effectively with German raids. In the east, the Roman proxy Odeanathus was thrashing the Persians on their own territory. Meanwhile, the Danube frontier was quiet. Did this mean peace for Rome at last?

The Goths Were Coming ...

Six centuries earlier Spartans and their allies had stood at Thermopylae and blocked the Persian advance into Greece. Ephialtes, the Greek traitor, had treacherously led the Persian troops along a goat-track that brought them directly behind the Spartan force. In 267 and 268 Goths on the shores of the Black Sea saw a way to avoid the entrenched legionary defences of the frontiers; they resolved to seize hundreds of ships and boats and use the seaways as a means to strike at the heart of the Roman Empire. This had never been done before. The first raiders beached their ships near Heraclea in northern Turkey and they began a campaign of plunder and destruction. Emperor Gallienus directed Odaenathus to halt his Persian war and to divert his army to Heraclea – the Goths had to be stopped. The Palmyrene lord did as he was asked but fell victim to aristocratic in-fighting. Odaenathus was murdered by one of his own kinsmen as part of some on-going domestic quarrel.

Early in 268 the adventurous Goths raided sites in the Balkans, they attacked Byzantium (with little success) and were able to sack the ancient cities of Corinth, Athens and Sparta. Although Gallienus managed to intercept the Goths and bring them to battle, little is known of the scale of his success. Greece represented the settled heartland of the Roman Empire, free from strife or terror. Gothic attacks on this scale and in this manner represented a new and terrifying form of warfare that the emperor and his legions had probably never imagined and had not planned for.

At a place called Nessus, probably in Macedonia, Gallienus engaged a Gothic army and slew 3,000 of them. This battle was not decisive and the emperor was forced to abandon his Balkan campaign to face yet another usurper – Aureolus had turned traitor once again. Declaring his support for Postumus and the Gallic empire, Aureolus marched on Italy with the imperial throne in his sights. With his Dalmatian cavalry Gallienus intercepted and defeated Aureolus' advance troops at Pontirolo in the north of Italy. Soon he had the rebel general besieged at Mediolanum (modern day Milan). During the siege, which lasted throughout the summer of 268, the emperor's senior officers seem to have begun conspiring against him. They waited until he was riding without his bodyguard, surrounded him and cut him down. His murder was not welcomed by the troops who complained bitterly that they had been robbed of a useful and indispensable emperor, a man who was 'courageous and competent.' Claudius, the commander of the cavalry wing, assumed the throne in his place.

At the moment that Gallienus met his end, the empire had never looked in a more precarious position. Gothic war bands were inside the borders and sacking prosperous Roman cities, the western provinces had seceded to create their own Gallic Empire and in the east, with Odaenathus dead, his widow Zenobia had taken control of Palmyra and its army. She was about to pursue her own interests, not those of Rome and was soon to carve away the eastern provinces to create an independent Palmyrene empire.

Little mention has been made of the plague which swept the cities intermittently, nor have the effects of rampant inflation been discussed, which caused misery and suffering for the citizens of even the most peaceful of regions. The year 268 truly marks the lowest point in Rome's history. Only a miracle could save the empire, that or an emperor of immense skill who could stitch the empire back together, drive out the barbarians and outfight and outlast the usurpers whose existence had become perhaps the only certainty of the third century.

Later Roman writers had few good things to say about Gallienus, repeating stories of his lecherousness and effeminacy and playing down his boundless energy, the victories that probably saved the total collapse of the empire, and his military reforms. Doubtless this slander was due to Gallienus' decision to prevent senators from serving as temporary military commanders. Instead he recruited tough and experienced officers who lacked titles, wealth and honours, but who came from a background of professional soldiering. Since many historians came from the senatorial class that was now barred from military service, there may have been some revenge to be had by blackening Gallienus' name.

Dura Europus

> 'Dura ... a foundation of the Macedonians, called Europos by the Greeks
> Isidore of Charax, Parthian Stations 4

In February 2012, French archaeologist Michael Landolt revealed the gruesome yet fascinating details of the First World War trench system that he had been digging. Located near Carspach in French Alsace, the timber-built underground shelter contained the bodies of 34 German soldiers who had all been killed when a French shell exploded above, causing the tunnels to collapse. The end came so quickly and the mud entombed the shelter's contents so thoroughly, that the grim scene was perfectly preserved ready for Landolt's diggers to unearth almost a century later.

Many of the soldiers were found in the positions they had been in at the very moment of the collapse, prompting some to liken the scene to Pompeii. Some of the skeletal remains were discovered sitting upright on a bench, whilst another was still laying where he died in his bed. One man was curled up in a foetal position at the bottom of a flight of stairs where he had been thrown by the blast. Along with the bodies were found a number of poignant personal artefacts including spectacles, wallets, pipes and wine bottles as well as the more utilitarian kit one would expect in a trench, such as rifles, ammunition, helmets and boots. However, although this montage represented a tiny part of a vast battle-front, its victims were known and could be identified. A nearby war memorial records their names and the date of their deaths.

Dura Europus, also likened to Pompeii, was a Syrian city located on the banks of the Euphrates river. In 255 or 256 it was besieged by the Persians and despite fierce Roman resistance its defences were breached. The military garrison as well as the civilian population were almost certainly deported to Persia. Other than the ruins of the fortifications, the buildings within them and the treasure trove of recovered artefacts, no record of this great event in the city's history survives. For the men and women struggling to defend Dura the siege was a momentous occasion; hundreds, perhaps thousands, of lives would have been lost in the struggle.

Once the city had fallen the Roman Empire ignored the loss and did not bother to repopulate the abandoned city. No mention is made of the siege in either Roman or Persian records. What a contrast to that single trench collapse at Carspach. Of course the Romans had no reason to crow about the defeat, many cities had fallen, Dura was but one more and Roman writers were always keen to avoid documenting defeats. The battle of Barballisos (252), for example, had been a crucial military confrontation involving tens of thousands of troops on both sides, yet because it was a humiliating defeat it received barely a mention in the annals.

Pompeii of the Syrian Desert

During the late 1920s and 1930s, a number of archaeologists, beginning with James Henry Breasted, worked at the site. Much of the later work was conducted by French and American teams and led first by Franz Cumont and later by Michael Rostovtzeff. It was Rostovtzeff who described Dura whimsically as 'the Pompeii of the Syrian Desert', a description which was ridiculed by his contemporaries because of the barren and forbidding appearance of the desert fortress.[5]

The city was important. It was built on an escarpment 90 m above the right bank of the Euphrates river and sat on the river frontier between Persia and Roman Syria, near the modern Syrian village of Salhiyé. One trade route snaked along the river bank all the way from Antioch to Ctesiphon, the Sassanid capital, another ran north to south from the great caravan city of Persian-aligned Hatra to the oasis town of Roman-aligned Palmyra. Once owned by the Parthians, it had been wrestled from them by the forces of Marcus Aurelius in 165 and had remained a Roman frontier town for almost a century.

A wealth of military equipment was discovered inside the ruined city, everything from sword blades to arrowheads, helmet fragments to horse armour. The dry desert conditions proved conducive to preservation and fragments of textiles, leather and wood were recovered by archaeologists during the 1930s. Finds are today scattered across several museums; most of the finds are held by Yale University Art Gallery, while the rest are found in the Damascus National Museum and the Royal Ontario Museum, Canada. Two pieces rest with the Louvre, in Paris.

For the study of the Roman military during the third century, the remains of Dura provide an invaluable treasure trove of information. Much of the assemblage resembles that of finds on the British, Rhine and Danubian frontiers, albeit in greater quantity. But Dura stands out for the unique survivals unknown anywhere else; papyrus documents give us the duty rosters of a garrison unit (*cohors* XX Palmyrenorum) and a fascinating wall painting depicts members of this actual unit attending a religious ceremony with their commander, Terentius. Other, equally stunning wall paintings survived on the walls of the synagogue at Dura, bringing us some of the colour and vibrancy of Roman life. A large number of intact Roman shields were also discovered, a find not equalled anywhere else

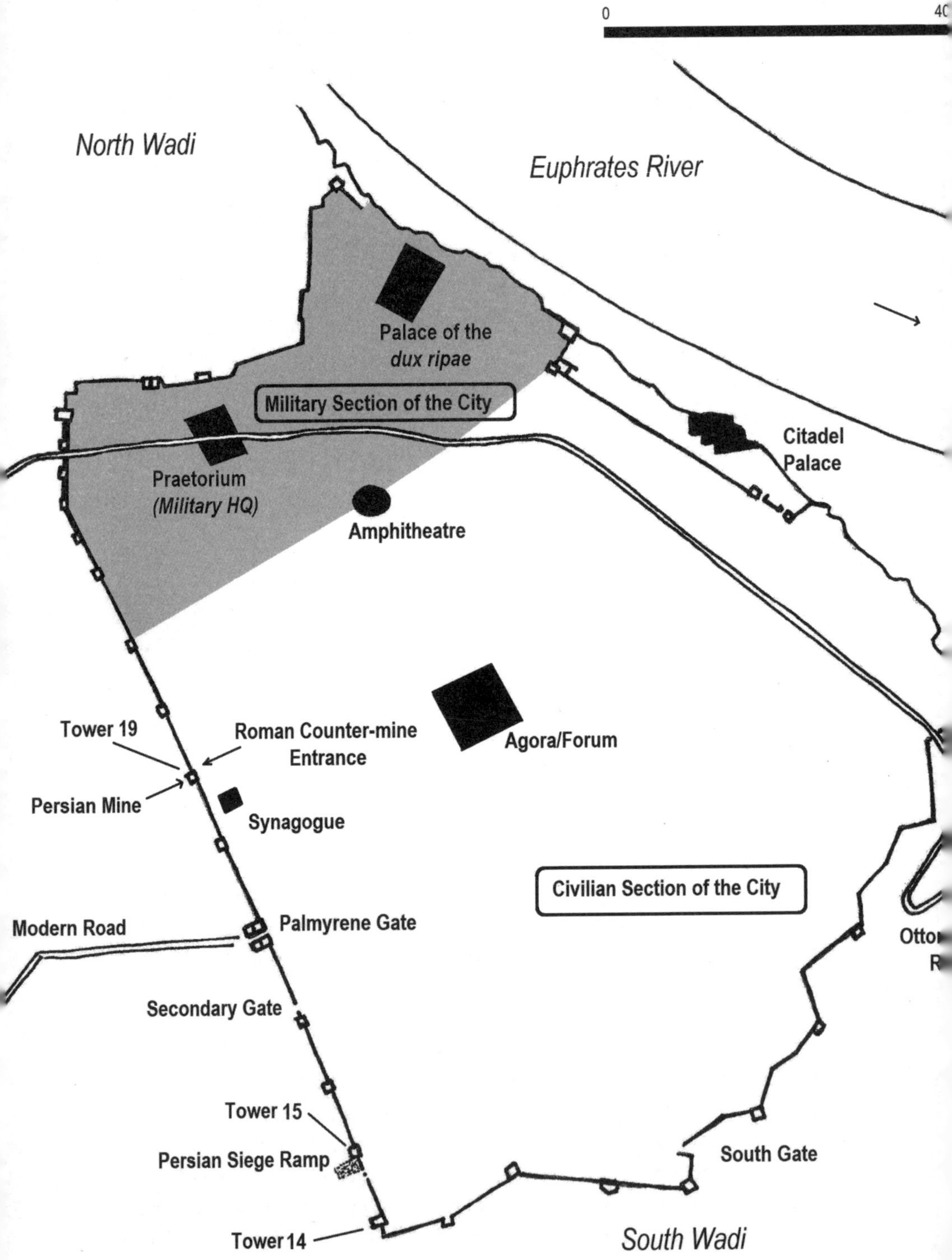
0
North Wadi
Euphrates River
Palace of the dux ripae
Military Section of the City
Citadel Palace
Praetorium (Military HQ)
Amphitheatre
Tower 19
Roman Counter-mine Entrance
Agora/Forum
Persian Mine
Synagogue
Civilian Section of the City
Modern Road
Palmyrene Gate
Secondary Gate
Tower 15
Persian Siege Ramp
South Gate
Tower 14
South Wadi

in the Roman Empire. Some still displayed their painted faces and together they provide a unique insight into Roman shield design.

Who Defended Dura Europus?

'Dura Europus' is a modern name, reflecting the city's complex past. Originally established by Greek-speakers, the city was known as Europos. Only later, when the fortress was built upon the escarpment to defend the site did the locals then refer to it instead as Dura ('fortress' in the local Semitic dialect).

Because of the city's crucial location and its distance from the Syrian governor and his legions, a regional commander called the *dux ripae* (commander of the river frontier) operated from Dura in the 240s and 250s. Under his command were both the forces stationed along the frontier as well as the garrison at Dura Europus. In the 240s this garrison had been *cohors* XX Palmyrenorum but it is unlikely to have still been in residence during the Persian siege.

A dramatic break occurred in the military garrison in 253 with Persians briefly taking control of the city. However, no signs of conflict were detected, leading archaeologists to conclude that the Roman garrison (the *cohors* XX) must have fled. Roman control was restored sometime in 254 as Valerian's expeditionary force began to aggressively engage Shapur's units that were dispersed throughout Syria.

A detachment of Legio IV Scythica was certainly present at around this time (a papyrus records a divorce of one of its legionaries in 254). Troops from nearby Palmyra are also likely to have been stationed in the city, supported no doubt by *vexillations* taken from legions brought to Syria by Valerian in 254. A fair estimate of the garrison strength ranges from 500 (a bare minimum) to 2,000 (the maximum based on available billets).[6]

The Siege

> Soon all the massed forces of the enemy were assaulting the city far more furiously than before ... we moved five of the lighter [ballista] to positions opposite the tower. These kept up a rapid fire of wooden projectiles, some of which transfixed two men at once.
>
> Ammianus Marcellinus, at the siege of Amida, 19.5

The city sits on an escarpment above the river Euphrates which runs east of the site. To the north and south are dry, desert gulleys (wadis) which provide a steep-sided defence. Only the westward side of the city is easily accessible, nevertheless the entire circuit of Dura was fortified with a substantial wall, reinforced by eleven towers and a strongly fortified central gateway.

In 255 or 256 a Persian army approached from the west and must have been challenged by Roman forces; scale horse-armour was discovered west of the wall with an arrowhead stuck in it. The main gate came under intensive attack and it is likely that once this failed, two simultaneous assaults were made on the western wall. One was directed at Tower 14, the second was focused on Tower 19. A siege tunnel was dug that began some 40 m west of Tower 19. The aim was to undermine the fortifications and then to set fire to the tunnel props, this would collapse not only the tunnel but also the tower and wall above it.

The tunnel reached beneath the tower and eventually side galleries were dug beneath the adjacent walls. The resulting spoil was heaped up as a defensive barrier around the mine entrance. In those last few days the Persian army would have waited expectantly for the tunnel to be completed, the troops watching basket after basket of earth come out of the tunnel. Within the city the legionaries must have seen the spoil heap growing larger and understood its meaning, they may even have heard the clink of iron tools below the walls. A counter-mine was hastily dug from inside the city to intercept the Persian tunnel and allow Roman soldiers to kill or drive off the Persian miners. *See* Colour Plate 25. The counter-mine was a success and hand-to-hand fighting took place. The bodies excavated from the tunnels indicate that *spatha*, javelins and oval shields were carried into the mines and that armour and cloaks were worn but that helmets were left behind. The Niederbieber-type helmet, with its deep neck guard, could not be used in a crouch position. The tunnel was around 1.6 m high and wide. Crowded with armed men in the dark, lit only by a couple of oil lamps or burning torches, it is hard to imagine the claustrophobic conditions and the terror of imminent combat as the iron picks broke through into a void. Persians would have been heard shouting warnings, there would be the flickering of enemy lamps and then hand-to-hand fighting once Persian soldiers were rushed down into the tunnel.

We know that the legionaries lost the fight, between sixteen and eighteen dead or wounded were left behind in the tunnel, they may have been overwhelmed by numbers or simply fled in fear from the confused mêlée and the prospect of being trapped in the dark to be butchered by the Persians. The tunnel must have been fired soon after and the Roman counter-mine was hastily blocked up by the panicked Roman defenders, terrified now that the Persians would use the Roman counter-mine to get inside Dura. Within the counter-mine the Persians were equally worried about a second Roman attack and they piled up the Roman dead into a heap against the face of the blocking wall.

One of the skeletons discovered by French excavators within this gruesome scene of tumbled bones, skulls and corroded military equipment, was Persian. He had been facing the city when he was wounded or killed and he fell on his back. Some attempt had been made by his comrades to drag him back to safety.

His ringmail shirt was pulled up about his neck as if a couple of rescuers had grabbed an arm each and a fistful of ringmail in their attempt to get him back to their own lines. Why was he left behind with the Roman dead? Perhaps the order to fire the mine had been given, perhaps they suddenly realised the soldier was dead. Much like the First World War skeletons discovered in the bunker at Alsace, those uncovered at Dura represent the final moments of some awful subterranean tragedy, a moment in a war that lasted several years, frozen in time for a later generation to wonder at and attempt to piece together.

Persian sappers set the counter-mine on fire then set about firing their own mine underneath Tower 19. Due to extensive reinforcement within the city, the walls did not fall forward and neither did Tower 19, instead both dropped vertically into the gap created by the collapsed tunnels. No breach in the wall occurred and the attack here was abandoned. The huge number of catapult and arrowheads found in the vicinity testify, however, to the ferocious missile exchanges going on throughout the mining attempt.

Attention probably shifted to Tower 14 and the southern end of the desert wall where another siege mine had also been excavated. The mine was fired and Tower 14 collapsed, rendering it useless as a Roman catapult platform. With this threat gone the Persian army then constructed a siege ramp from debris, rocks and soil that would allow its troops to march right up to the Roman ramparts. At the same time a tunnel was dug beneath the siege ramp to lead underneath the walls. Much wider than the mine of Tower 19, this tunnel was probably intended to allow Persian assault troops into the city when the grand attack began. It failed because the defenders again dug a counter-mine and this time successfully captured the Persian tunnel. It was then used to create sabotage tunnels inside the siege ramp which caused parts of it to collapse. At this point the mining seems to have stopped. It may be that the Persians were able to take back their attack tunnel and use the Roman counter-mine to get inside Dura, seizing the city for themselves. There is no evidence of fighting and it could be that the inhabitants surrendered once the enemy gained entry. The stones are mute. No written records exist to explain the sequence of events or the dramatic outcome. Everything has had to be pieced together by archaeologists and historians living centuries after the fact.

The weeks or months of resistance and furious digging were at an end, the city was looted and everyone in it herded together and led east into Persia. Evidence suggests that many thousands of Roman captives lived out their lives in Iran during this period, building bridges and cities and perhaps even carving the famous Naqsh-e Rustam relief that commemorates Shapur's victory over the Roman general Valerian.

10

Restitutor Orbis

'Aurelian might now congratulate the senate, the people and himself that, in a little more than three years, he had restored universal peace and order to the Roman world.'

Edward Gibbon, *The History of the Decline and Fall of the Roman Empire*

Rome had faced difficult times before. In the third century BC, Hannibal had led an army into Italy and inflicted crushing defeats on the legions sent against it. Four centuries before, however, Rome was one power amongst many clustered around the Mediterranean, all of them vying for supremacy.

Now, in 268, the great Roman superpower that dominated western Europe and the Mediterranean had been torn in three, was ravaged by plague (probably smallpox), suffered from crippling inflation and almost constant invasion from the north or the east. What is more, an emperor had been captured and enslaved. Ironically, any general capable of dealing with the military threat quickly took the opportunity to seize the throne. New generals, flushed with a victory whilst fighting for this new emperor saw how easily power could be achieved and inevitably made their own bid for the throne. Set on this course, with a cycle of assassinations and military coups eating up the vital energy of Rome, the outcome looked hopeless.

What If? The End of Rome

Imagine for a moment that the fragmented Roman Empire, cut apart by Zenobia and Postumus, was never reunited. No strong man came forward in the 270s to bring the rebel provinces to heel. What would have been the Fate of Rome? Most likely other regions and in particular the Danubian provinces (including Greece, Pannonia and Moesia) would have gone the way of the Gallic Empire. They might have declared their own emperor, one who they trusted to stay away from Rome in order to strengthen the defences of the region. In the east Palmyra would retain control of Syria, Asia Minor, Libya and Egypt; in the west the Gallic

Empire would continue to hold Britain, Gaul and the Rhine garrisons. Spain may have gone over to the central power, Italy, along with its loyal and wealthy provinces in North Africa and Sicily. Between the Alps and the Hellespont a new 'Danubian Empire' would attempt to keep the Goths at bay.

This 'regionalisation' mirrors the historical state of affairs that existed at the end of the third century when the emperor Diocletian consciously split the empire four-ways in order to improve local defence and reduce the communication lag between the centre and the periphery. Diocletian's imperial districts match those of our hypothetical independent empires.

Perhaps this arrangement might have lasted five years, ten years or thirty. Like the Successor kingdoms that Alexander's generals carved out of his empire after 323 BC, they would certainly make war on one another and contend the ownership of marginal provinces and territories. We can, for example, imagine the Gallic Empire willing to spill blood in order to regain Spain and Italy eager to see itself reunited with the Danube region. Whatever the relationship between these fragments of empire might be, the threat of the Goths and Persians was not about to go away. Zenobia might be able to keep the Sassanid Persians at bay for some time but inevitably by the end of the third century if not before, that aggressive empire would swing in to take the east from her. Egypt and Syria might easily have fallen permanently into the hands of the Persians.

Goths would inevitably apply crippling pressure to the Danubian kingdom and make violent forays into Italy too. Perhaps the Goths could be persuaded, as they were a century later, to fight for pay, to turn mercenary and vent their fury upon a rival imperial power. Certainly the Goths would take advantage of Rome's weakened state to loot and pillage vulnerable cities at every opportunity, laying waste to entire regions if not checked by military force. If one or more of the tribal chiefs decide to settle permanently within the Roman provinces, then client kingdoms may spring up, similar to those of western Europe in the early fifth century. The Goths are likely to gut Italy and perhaps set up their own Gothic kingdoms. In essence we would see an accelerated collapse of the empire due to overwhelming barbarian pressure, not just in the west as in the historical fifth century, but in the east too. There would be no eastern Roman Empire to survive the historical fall of the west and, by extension, no Byzantium. What the implications of *that* would be cannot be explored here.

Claudius Gothicus

> Both the senate and people held him in such affection both before his rule and during his rule and after his rule that ... neither Trajan nor any of the Antonines nor any other emperor was so beloved.
>
> Historia Augusta, *The Life of Claudius*

Rome did not collapse in the 270s. This was only due to the extraordinary actions of two emperors, both of whom originated in Illyria (the region encompassing the former Yugoslavia). They were to be the first of a long line of tough soldier emperors from Illyria that had the determination and the ability to restore the empire. The first of these men was Claudius II who immediately succeeded Gallienus in September 268. Claudius was commander of a reserve force at Ticinum (modern Pavia) at the time of Gallienus' assassination but he had held several notable military commands in the past and seemed a natural candidate for the throne.

Once the usurper Aureolus had been dealt with at Milan, Claudius had to march north in order to counter a large invasion of Alemanni that had broken into Italy through the Alps. At Lake Garda these barbarians were decisively defeated. Within months, however, the new emperor had taken up the Gothic campaign begun by his predecessor and began to harry the Gothic tribes that had invaded Pannonia *en masse*. The crucial battle was fought at Naissus (modern Niš in Serbia) a bloody affair costing tens of thousands of Gothic lives. Roman soldiers enjoyed their share of the captured plunder that had been looted by the Goths. The campaign continued throughout 269 and 270 with the Gothic remnant eventually finding itself isolated in the Balkan Mountains. Suffering from hunger, plague, desertion and combat losses the Goths were in poor shape and were unable to stand against Claudius. For his military successes in the Balkans, the emperor won the appellation 'Claudius Gothicus'.[1]

The plague that afflicted the enemy took its toll on the Roman army too. At Sirmium in August 270, the emperor Claudius himself became one of its many victims. He had been a tough, no nonsense professional soldier known for his integrity, height and strength (and also his ability to punch a horse and knock out its teeth!). The Gothic victory earned Claudius his fame, but of equal importance for the future of the Roman Empire was the expeditionary force sent west by him in 269. This army took back southern Gaul from the Gallic emperor Victorinus. At around the same time Spain left the Gallic Empire and renewed its allegiance with Rome. Although these western achievements did not restore the empire, they did begin the process of reunification that would be completed by the commander of the Dalmatian cavalry, a man called Lucius Domitius Aurelianus ('Aurelian').

The Aurelian Wall

Claudius had a brother, Quintillus, who briefly held the throne in September 270. He was based in the city of Aquileia to organise the defence of northern Italy. When he heard that the Danubian legions had proclaimed Aurelian as emperor, Quintillus committed suicide.

Now Aurelian faced the task of trying to piece together the empire. Before he could take action, though, he was forced to react to yet another border invasion, this time by a new Germanic group called the Vandals. After crossing the Danube, the tribe looted territories around Aquincum (modern Budapest). It was soon engaged in a protracted winter campaign against Aurelian's forces and the emperor attempted to deny food and shelter to the barbarians by employing a harsh 'scorched earth' policy. Forcing the Vandals back across the Danube in 271, Aurelian then defeated them in battle. Remarkably, he offered the Vandals safe passage home if they agreed to provide him with hostages as well as the use of two thousand Sarmatian cavalrymen that had accompanied the tribe.

As the agreed withdrawal began, news soon arrived that more Germans, this time the Alemanni, had carried out a lightning attack on northern Italy. Torn between two foes, Aurelian decided to remain in Pannonia with his elite troops while the bulk of the imperial field army marched quickly to Italy's rescue. Once he was sure that the Vandals would not return, the emperor caught up with his army.

Italy once again suffered the pain, humiliation and destruction wrought by a Germanic invasion. In 259 the Alemanni had reached as far as Milan before being repulsed and in 268 they had penetrated the Alps a second time. These earlier raids had been stopped in northern Italy, but the force now facing Aurelian beat back his army and, breaking into smaller groups, pushed on towards Rome. The city of Placentia (modern Piacenza) was sacked by the Alemanni but the raiders were eventually defeated in a series of battles that exposed the terrible vulnerability of the Roman capital. Aurelian shadowed the Alemanni through Italy, finally catching and defeating them at Ticinum (modern Pavia) as they tried to leave Italy with their loot.

In recognition of the danger facing Rome, Aurelian immediately commissioned the building of a wall around the city. This would be a stupendous undertaking but was nevertheless completed in under six years. The 'Aurelian Wall' had a circuit of 19 km and enclosed all of Rome's most important buildings, an area of some 2,500 hectares. The wall protected the heart of the city as well as the key Tiber bridges and it included in its circuit the Praetorian Camp. Practical considerations forced short-cuts; the wall's builders were civilians and they worked in concrete and brick using methods familiar to them. Soldiers from the legions could be spared neither for its construction, nor for its defence. Where possible, existing monumental buildings were incorporated into the defences, including the Amphitheatre Castrense, the tomb of the baker Eurysaces, the side of a tenement block, the Praetorian Camp and even the Pyramid (and tomb) of Caius Cestius.

Standing before the Aurelian Wall today, one cannot fail to be impressed by the tremendous scale of the fortification. Well preserved sections still tower to a height of 8 m (including the battlements that once protected the rampart-walk) and in places it is more than 3.5 m thick. Towers project from the face of the wall at regular intervals (typically less than 30 m apart) and these served primarily as artillery platforms. Roman artillery of the day consisted of twin-armed torsion *ballista*, designed to launch iron-headed darts out to a range in excess of 200 m. There were 381 of these simple rectangular towers along the wall's circuit (although Rome could never have mustered an equivalent number of trained *ballistarii* teams to man them all) and these towers rose another 4.5 m above the height of the curtain wall. *See* Colour Plate 29.

Access through the Aurelian Wall was gained through one of eighteen gateways, four of these, the Porta Flaminia, Porta Appia, Porta Portuensis and Porta Ostiensis East, served as Rome's main thoroughfares. They all featured double-span archways and were flanked by impressive, round-fronted towers. Other gateways (such as Porta Tiburtina and Porta Latina) were only built with single-span arches but they too were flanked by round-fronted towers. These city gates sat across roads of secondary importance.

The wall served as 'a formidable barrier not a fighting platform'.[2] Against a concerted attack from an enemy versed in siege-craft, such as the Persians, the Aurelian Wall would have been an easy nut to crack. It was intended, however, to protect Rome from a sudden attack by a barbarian force until a relief force from northern Italy or the Danube frontier could reach the city. Goths and Germans alike had shown little ability in siege warfare which is understandable for cultures that possessed no cities of their own.

The construction of the Aurelian Wall marks a low ebb in the history of the empire. Italy and Rome were not safe and the imperial field army could no longer guarantee the security of Rome's inhabitants. Aurelian's building of the wall was certainly necessary but it also proclaimed the vulnerability of Rome in the face of unrelenting barbarian aggression. Should faith in the Aurelian Walls waver, the next step would surely have been to shift the capital further away from the vulnerable northern borders, to a place more easily defensible. Around fifty years later, with the founding of Constantinople by emperor Constantine in 330, this is exactly what happened.

The War Against Palmyra

The year 268 had seen the assassination of both emperor Gallienus as well as his ally in the east, Odaenathus, ruler of Palmyra. While Gallienus was succeeded by Claudius II, Odaenathus left his kingdom to his young son Vaballathus and his wife, the queen Zenobia. Despite continuing with the pretence of owing fealty to Rome, this ambitious woman planned to seize the eastern provinces in order that she might create a powerful and independent Palmyrene empire.

In 269 her fast moving armies captured Palestine, parts of Asia Minor, Egypt, Syria and Antioch. Although the oasis city of Palmyra was small by imperial standards and unable to support a large army, Zenobia was able to co-opt the broken and dispirited Roman forces of the region, offering them strong, local leadership and a proven track record of victories against the Persians. Of her own forces, the most numerous were the horse archers, while the most effective in close combat were the cataphracts. This heavy cavalry force armed with long-swords and lances was devastating in the charge and almost invulnerable – both horse and rider were completely clad in mail or scale armour.

Up until late 271, his attention focused on Gothic and Germanic invasions, Aurelian had been forced to accept Vaballathus as his imperial colleague in the east. Now that these matters had been taken care of, the emperor marched east in an attempt to take back the eastern provinces. Gothic aggression flared up in the Balkans in the spring of 272, however, forcing Aurelian to change his priorities yet again. Fierce fighting ended with a Roman victory against the Gothic king Cannabas, but nevertheless the emperor decided to reduce the length of the frontier in that region. Beyond the Danube frontier lay Dacia, the province conquered by emperor Trajan 170 years earlier. It had been colonised, Romanised and garrisoned by imperial legions, but in recent decades had become a salient, a vulnerable territory that was increasingly difficult to protect and surrounded by hostile tribes on three sides.

Dacia was abandoned to the barbarians, a bold move that would require the evacuation of tens of thousands of civilians and soldiers along with their possessions. Aurelian 'removed the Romans from the Dacian cities and fields and gathered them together in the middle of Moesia, calling that Dacia,' While he remained to oversee the operation, the emperor sent one of his generals, Marcus Aurelius Probus, to retake Egypt from Zenobia. Commanding a large fleet of warships, Probus was able to reunite Egypt with Rome once again. Dacia had been lost, permanently, but at the same time the recapture of Egypt outweighed that loss and increased Aurelian's prestige.[3]

When the imperial army arrived in Asia Minor, garrisons soon began to defect to Aurelian and most of the cities welcomed him. The first major battle of the campaign took place in May 272 at Immae some 40 km east of Antioch; Zenobia could not afford to lose control of this key strategic city. Unable to adequately respond to the threat posed by the superb Palmyrene heavy cavalry, Aurelian attempted to lure it away from the battlefield. This stratagem worked, tiring the cataphracts to such an extent that they were slaughtered by an ambush of faster moving Roman cavalry. Antioch was back under Roman control and the emperor spent some months at the city.

Zenobia had escaped to fight again and a second battle was fought later in the year at Emesa (modern Homs). Again the Palmyrene heavy cavalry proved to be a worry for the Romans, indeed, a feigned retreat turned into a near disaster as the eastern cataphracts actually caught up with the Roman cavalry. Following the charge when Aurelian saw that the feared Palmyrene horsemen were disordered and milling about, he decided to swing his legionary infantry around and attack the enemy. Using *pilum* and sword the Roman foot soldiers engaged the cataphracts and auxiliary troops from Palestine, armed with maces, moved forward to club the well-armoured horsemen to death.

Emesa proved to be another Roman victory and the decisive battle of the Palmyrene War. Queen Zenobia fled back to Palmyra with the remnants of her army to await the inevitable arrival of Aurelian. The hot, Arabian summer of 272 soon saw the oasis city under siege and it ended with the capture of the queen as she tried to flee to Persia. Aurelian was magnanimous in victory and did not destroy the city or enslave its inhabitants. A year later, however, the emperor was forced to return when the Palmyrenes rose in revolt to support a usurper called Septimius Antiochus. Aurelian sacked the city and dismantled its fortifications. This marked the end for proud Palmyra and it was gradually abandoned, leaving only ruins in the desert.

Queen Zenobia was brought back to Rome in chains by the emperor in order that she be paraded in his triumph through the city. Her ultimate Fate is not certain, although one account has her living out her life in luxury at Tibur (modern Tivoli, 30 km north east of Rome). According to the writer Eutropius, 'Zenobia left descendants at Rome who still live there.'[4]

Recovery of the West

Aurelian did not stop. His successes in battle fostered loyalty amongst his legions and without the distraction of a civil war he could now turn west to address the breakaway Gallic Empire. Gaius Esuvius Tetricus was the current Gallic emperor and like those before him, his strength rested on the might of the garrisons in Britain and on the Rhine.

In the spring of 274, Aurelian made his play, crossing the Alps at a smart pace and entering the Gallic province of Narbonensis (roughly equivalent to the modern Languedoc region of France). His march into northern Gaul was rapid and many towns surrendered to Aurelian's forces without a fight. Tetricus, gambling on the loss of Gaul to gain him time, had been mobilising the Rhine legions.

The two emperors met one another at the head of their battle-hardened legions at the Catalaunian Fields (modern Châlons-en-Champagne). The death toll was high, these soldiers knew their trade. Tetricus and his son were both captured during the battle but spared by Aurelian. Both the Gallic emperor and Zenobia appeared in his triumph through Rome later that year and, like Zenobia, Tetricus and his son were allowed to keep their lives, indeed they were granted official positions. By the end of 274, Britain, Gaul and the German provinces were once more reunited with the rest of the Roman Empire. It was whole again for the first time in almost fifteen years.

The bitter legacy of the Châlons victory was a desperate reduction in the effectiveness of the Rhineland legions. As a result, less than twenty-four months later the Alemanni and the Franks would smash through the weakened frontier in a concerted attack. For Aurelian the future still looked hopeful, the empire had been restored and he had been justly awarded the title of *restitutor orbis* (Restorer of the World). Shapur, the king of Persia who had been the bane of Rome for decades, had died early on in Aurelian's reign. One son, then another, reigned in his stead and this period of transition provided Rome with valuable breathing space in the east.[5]

After defeating another invasion by Germanic tribes in 275, the emperor began to plan for an expedition against Persia. *En route* to Antioch, however, Aurelian was assassinated by the Praetorian Guard, most likely because of the strict anti-corruption legislation that he had introduced in an effort to stabilise the economy. He was buried with great ceremony by his legions near Perinthus, on the Bosphorus (modern Marmara Ereğlisi in Turkey). An emperor who paid off his enemies (Alexander Severus) or suffered defeat on the battlefield (Gordian III) was held in contempt by his soldiers; an emperor who knew victory was loved.

The senate deified Aurelian and few other third century emperors deserved that honour more than he. One can ask the question 'what would have happened if he had survived longer?' about every emperor, but with Aurelian that question has real meaning. With the backing of the senate and the legions, and with Persia at a low ebb, Aurelian may have been able to make a real difference. He had certainly showed some interest in tackling Rome's terrible economic situation.

Six Emperors

Between the death of Aurelian in 275 and the accession of Diocletian in 284 there would be six incumbents on the throne. Only one, Marcus Aurelius Probus, lasted more than a couple of years, and all but one fell victim to assassination. Yet each played their part in maintaining the security of the frontiers, preventing barbarian incursions and the secession of provinces that were unhappy with rule from Rome. Unusually, the choice of the next emperor was not made by the soldiers or their commanders as had become the norm. In 275 a letter was sent from Aurelian's troops to the senate asking them to nominate a suitable candidate. The man they chose was Marcus Claudius Tacitus, an elderly member of the senate and an Italian by birth. It is likely that he had a military background and was already known to the legions.

Tacitus joined the army already assembled by Aurelian in order to lead it first into Asia Minor and then on to Syria to make war on Persia. After crossing the Bosphorus he led the troops in battle against a Gothic tribe, earning himself the title of 'Gothicus Maximus'. Later in 276 Tacitus was murdered in Cappadocia (modern southern Turkey) after a reign of only six months. It seems that his son, Maximinus, had made himself unpopular through exactions in Syria. Florianus, a relative of Tacitus and the incumbent praetorian commander, took control.

Florianus engaged the Goths in Asia Minor once again but was robbed of victory by a rebellion breaking out further south. Marcus Aurelius Probus was a commander on the eastern frontier who had garnered the support of Egypt, Syria and the rest of the eastern provinces. The clash of legions, those of Florianus from the west and those of Probus from the east, faced one another at Tarsus, close to the Syrian border. Disease, the heat of summer and skirmishing seriously affected the morale of the emperor's troops. It was a group of soldiers from the army of Probus who convinced the western legions to kill Florianus. He had reigned for only eighty-eight days.

Probus was, like Aurelian and Claudius Gothicus, an Illyrian and a professional soldier born in Sirmium. This was fortunate, for the man spent his entire six year reign struggling to defend the empire from a renewed torrent of aggressors. The Rhine legions, understrength and demoralised from their defeat at the battle of Châlons in 274, could not hold back the ferocious German attacks on Gaul. The devastation in this region, wrought by tribes such as the Franks, Burgundians and Vandals was unprecedented. For two years Probus fought these invaders and was eventually able to restore the frontier on both the Rhine and the upper Danube. Manpower shortages must have been a pressing problem.

Further campaigns were fought in 279 on the lower Danube, in Asia Minor and in Egypt. As if these were not taxing enough, the emperor also faced a pair of usurpers, joint emperors from Colonia Claudia Ara Agrippinensium (modern Cologne). There were other challengers, too, both the governor of Syria and the governor of Britain launched their own rebellions. Probus successfully dealt with these usurpers, but the lure of an eastern campaign in spring, 282, proved the undoing of him. His own praetorian prefect, Marcus Aurelius Carus, used the opportunity to launch a bid for the throne. This rebel was backed by the tough legions of the Danube frontier and their disloyalty spread quickly to other parts of the army; Probus was murdered by his own troops close to Sirmium in the 'Iron Tower'.

The Fate of the empire now rested in the hands of Carus, a member of the professional officer corps and his two sons, Carinus and Numerian. Carus had the foresight to share power with his sons, eventually giving Carinus the rank of Augustus (joint emperor) and Numerian the rank of Caesar (junior emperor). After tackling Sarmatians and Quadi on the Danube Carus took his armies, and his younger son Numerian, east into Persia. There they marched through Mesopotamia, defeated the Persians in battle and even captured Ctesiphon, a feat not equalled by a Roman leader since the days of Septimius Severus.

> Carus, born at Narbo, ruled two years. He immediately made Carinus and Numerian Caesars. He died near Ctesiphon by the blow of a lightning bolt.
>
> Aurelius Victor, *Epitome de Caesaribus*, 38

The death of Carus in 283 remains a mystery. Was he killed by lightning while camping amidst his troops on the banks of the Tigris? Was he assassinated? Perhaps the lightning bolt was a metaphor for some divine judgement. However he met his end, it was Numerian, the younger son and junior partner, who inherited the Roman Empire.

With the Persians defeated, Numerian ordered the Roman expedition to withdraw. He was ill and wintered in Syria, moving on through Asia Minor the following year. Thc emperor had been blinded by an eye disease whilst on campaign in the desert and travelled within a closed litter. Here, set apart from his men, Numerian was murdered by his father-in-law, Lucius Flavius Aper, commander of the Praetorians. In a gruesome turn of events the body was not discovered immediately. The litter was carried towards the Bosphorus day after day and the murder only discovered once the stink of the corpse could no longer be concealed.

At Nicomedia, Aper's part in the crime was discovered and during a military trial he was struck down and killed by Diocletian, the commander of the imperial guard cavalry. (the *protectores domestici*, or household cavalry). Diocletian claimed the throne for himself, yet he still faced Carinus, the elder son of Carus who was ruling in the west. In the summer of 285 the forces of Carinus and Diocletian met on the banks of the river Margus (Morava) near the Roman city of Singidunum (modern Belgrade). Although it looked as though Carinus might win through, an officer with a grudge assassinated him on the battlefield, handing victory to Diocletian. The legions that had backed Carinus now transferred their allegiance to the usurper – a usurper like no other.

Diocletian would finally break the deadly cycle of assassination and usurpation that had plagued the third century. It is during his long rule that the Roman Empire (as well as the Roman army) would be totally remade. Perhaps Aurelian could have steered the empire out of trouble given time, perhaps Tacitus or Claudius Gothicus could have done the same but they had fallen before their true potential could be realised. Diocletian, however, was able to keep a grip on power for two decades, giving him the time he needed to change what he needed in order to save the Roman Empire and finally end the third century crisis.

11

Epilogue: Into the Fourth Century

'[Diocletian] was a very industrious and capable emperor,'

Eutropius, *Breviarium, 9*

It is impossible to underestimate the crucial role played by Diocletian in the history of Rome. One measure of his impact is that some medieval historians look upon 284 and the accession of Diocletian as the start of the medieval period. Yale University, for example, currently offers a course called 'The Early Middle Ages: 284-1000'.

This man had a long-range vision for the empire, not based on traditional systems and institutions, but on what worked. He formalised the trend that had grown throughout the third century for autocratic government and he developed a political system for power sharing that recognised the impossibility of one man administering and defending such a large and vulnerable territory as the Roman Empire.

Taxes went up but the overburdened Roman taxpayer got a lot for his money; the civil service was greatly expanded and the army was doubled in size. Of course this last measure was a reaction to the continual state of war that the frontier troops now found themselves in. In addition, many troops, located far from their bases and operating in mixed *vexillations* found themselves 'incorporated' - the entire *ad hoc* unit becoming a permanent military regiment stationed where it was currently located. In this way hundreds of new units, each with a headcount far less than a traditional legion, sprang into being. This was military 'rationalisation'.

The enlarged civil service was used to collect and process the huge revenues now needed in order to pay for the army. Exactions were often in kind – food, clothing and other goods going directly to the troops (often via extortionate means). Diocletian's Rome was a totalitarian military state. The crossbow brooch, first worn by soldiers in the early third century and soon adopted by them as a mark of status, became almost a symbol of the new military regime. In Diocletian's new state it was not only soldiers who wore the heavy military brooch but also members of the government and the civil service. In a world where military uniforms as such did not exist, the crossbow brooch signified political and military authority and became a badge of status.

Similarly in dictatorships around the world today that are backed up by military force , the dictator himself and doubtless his sons and advisors show a preference for military uniforms, whether or not they have spent any time within the armed forces.

Diocletian made reforms at all levels. State factories were established for the production of weaponry, armour and textiles since their supply had to be both reliable and available in great quantities. He subdivided the provinces of the empire in order to better secure closer financial control. He multiplied the numbers of secret police, of informers and spies in order to maintain control of his new authoritarian state.

Perhaps Diocletian's greatest effect on the life of the average Roman citizen was his decision to force the rural population to remain where they were and bind them to the land. Soon, any landowner who even suspected that his tenant farmers wanted to escape had the right to chain them. This was the beginning of medieval serfdom. It was not just agricultural workers but miners, arms manufacturers, soldiers, civil servants and members of the imperial mints, the postal service and even the gravediggers, that were all legally bound to their jobs. What was more, their sons were obliged to follow in their father's footsteps.

This ancient totalitarian state based on crippling taxation provided the funds needed for a massive defensive army. Decades of experience in the third century had shown that the thirty-three current legions and their associated auxiliary regiments had just not been able to maintain the integrity of the empire. It was one thing to plan this great autocracy and to propose grandiose plans for the expansion of the army and the taxation system that would support it, but how could one guarantee to be alive long enough to see the reforms through to their end? Just look at the year 284 ... emperors Carinus and Numerian were both killed, and Diocletian took the throne. Emperor Carus had only been killed the year before. Look at the year 270 ... three emperors ruled the empire one after another; Claudius, his brother Quintillus and finally Aurelian.

To secure his survival, Diocletian instituted the Tetrarchy. This unique experiment in power-sharing involved four emperors dividing the provinces up between themselves in order that each might govern his own sector. To reduce the chance of civil war and the threat of usurpation, each emperor also nominated a junior partner who became that emperor's successor. The system provided stability for over twenty years which was enough time for Diocletian to fully develop his military dictatorship.

The Tetrarchy had begun as joint-rule in 286 when Diocletian elevated the general Maximian to the post of co-emperor. While Diocletian administered the west, Maximian ruled the east. In 293 the system was widened to include two junior emperors, Galerius and Constantius Chlorus. Eight years later the senior emperors jointly abdicated to enter retirement of their own free will, allowing Constantius and Galerius to step into their positions as senior co-emperors (Augustii). As expected, they appointed two new junior emperors (Caesars): Flavius Valerius

Severus in the west under Constantius, and Maximinus in the east under Galerius. This logical system depended on the tacit agreement of those involved ... should one man not hold to his place in the system, things were to go awry.

The Tetrarchy did not survive intact, yet it was tacit recognition that the empire no longer belonged to one man: power *had* to be shared. Of course there had been co-emperors before, Marcus Aurelius had shared power with Lucius Verus, Severus with his son Caracalla, and Valerian with his own son, Gallienus. The way in which power was shared varied widely during these earlier times, depending on circumstance and current events. However, the system that grew out of the Tetrarchy and that lasted throughout the fourth and fifth centuries, recognised the formal division of the Roman empire into two halves, east and west, governed by two emperors of equal status and power.

Diocletian and his co-emperors presided over a 'rationalisation' of the Roman military. Not only was it greatly expanded and the use of *vexillations* brought to an end with the creation of more and smaller forces but the weaponry and armour used changed also. Expensive and complex items of equipment seem to have made it no further than the last quarter of the third century. *Lorica segmentata* vanishes from both the archaeological as well as the representational record and so too does the plywood rectangular shield that had once been synonymous with the legions. Gone, also is the expensive riveted and tanged *pilum* in favour of a range of lighter javelins including the barbed-head *spiculum* and the weighted throwing dart, the *plumbata*.[1]

Under this money-saving revision, manufacture of the heavy and expensive helmets of the third century, the Niederbieber and Heddernheim types, was stopped. Instead new helmets were introduced, cheaply made and quick to produce they were of composite construction. The bowl of the helmet was no longer one piece but two, attached together by a rigid strip running from the front to the back of the helm. Separate neck guards and cheek pieces were not attached with hinges, as previously but simply hung from leather straps. More than a dozen helmets of this type were found at Intercisa in Hungary and the design is also found in fourth century representations. Some ridge helmets were composed of more than two parts and a few others were elaborately decorated. Yet they were all relatively cheap and easy to make and epitomise the logistical necessities of Diocletian's new age.[2]

Although the Roman military may have expanded and cut costs where it could during Diocletian's reign, the way it fought had been perfected over a hundred years of almost constant warfare. The third century crisis had forced the men of the legions to change both their kit and the way in which they fought. It was this method of combat, using the spear, long sword and oval shield, that would come to dominate legionary warfare for the next two hundred years. By the time of emperor Maurice, around 600, cavalry had become the main arm of the Roman army and at that point, one may argue, the day of the legionary soldier was at an end.

Appendix: Additional Detail for Some of the Colour Plates

Plate 1: Soldiers on the Column of Marcus Aurelius (AD 180). The Column displays a mix of shield shapes as well as the continued use of *lorica hamata* and *lorica segmentata.*

Plate 2: Arch of Septimius Severus in the Imperial Forum, Rome. The arch was dedicated by Severus in 204 to commemorate his recent victories against Parthia. Today it dominates the Forum and stands close to the Senate House (*curia*) built by Emperor Diocletian.

Plate 3: Part of a banquet scene on a wall painting from Komárom (Brigetio) in Hungary. Wall painting showing two people at a banquet. Both of the mens' tunics clearly show the typical arrow-shaped *clavii* decoration that was popular throughout the third century.

Plate 4: Husband and wife on a tombstone from Augsburg. This tombstone shows clearly everyday dress and appearance of an off-duty soldier and his wife. There were variations of third century belt, but this one is typical, the two ends of the belt feed through the ring and fold back to be held in place by mushroom-shaped studs. The leather belt ends are pierced with slits which allow the studs to pass through. Variations of this belt abounded.

Plate 5 : Painted tile depicting Heliodorus, a military accountant from Dura Europus. This painted tile from the House of the Scribes depicts an *actuarius* or military finance officer, his name is Heliodorus. The vivid colours help us understand the appearance of a third century soldier. His cloak is pale brown, his tunic white with a neck-line of pinkish-red (originally purplish-red when found). A short-cropped beard and moustache typify the third century 'look'.

Plate 6: Soldier 'Out-of-armour'. Images on third century gravestones as well as the Terentius wall-painting are used to create the impression of a soldier 'out of armour'. He wears a white woollen tunic decorated with *clavii*, dark blue footed trousers and boots based on a find from Saalburg, Germany. The cloak is held by a crossbow brooch, attested at many sites, and his sword is held by a wide baldric, decorated with Zugmentel-style open-work fittings. The belt ends in two metal terminals and the soldier 'plays' with these, just as soldiers are seen doing on several gravestones.

Plate 7: Soldier in Ringmail. A typical armed and armoured third century legionary. His iron and brass helmet is a Niederbieber type and his ringmail shirt descends to mid-thigh. The neck is protected with a scale gorget, his legs by iron greaves. He still wears the ring buckle belt and sword baldric, the sword hangs on the left, behind the shield. He fights with a 2.5 metre-long spear and this example is a reproduction of a find from Künzing. The oval shield is based on several finds from Dura Europus, its blue reverse face motif is a copy of that found on shield 617.

Plate 8: Soldier in *lorica segmentata*. While 7 represents the new look legionary, this soldier retains much of the equipment from the second century. He wears an old-style *lorica segmentata* over a leather *subarmalis* complete with strips of thigh protection (*pteruges*). He cradles the Niederbieber helmet in his right arm and holds a light *pilum* in his left. Behind the soldier is the classic Roman *scutum*, although this example is a copy of one found at Dura Europus; it has rawhide edging rather than brass, and is fitted with a four-rivet, rectangular brass umbo ('boss') which was missing from the original.

Plate 9: Lanciarius. The gravestones of Legio II Parthica included those of *lanciarii*, 'legionary javelin-men' like Aurelius Mucianus. With a requirement for speed and mobility, this *lanciarii* wears only a Von Kalkar-Hoenepel-style helmet for protection. His hat is felted wool and resembles an arming cap found at Dura Europus. He still carries a *spatha* for hand-to-hand combat, but his primary weapon is a clutch of short javelins. These may have been carried in a long quiver as depicted here, alternatively four or five javelins may have been held in the shield hand whilst throwing with the right arm.

Plate 10: Soldier With Drawn *spatha*. Despite the adoption of spears and short javelins by the legionaries, the expensive, pattern-welded *spatha* remained the primary killing weapon. Here the soldier fights over his oval shield with his sword, something earlier, *gladius*-equipped legionaries would have found difficult. He wears *lorica segmentata* over a leather *subarmalis* and an Imperial Italic H type helmet, it retains the appearance of earlier Roman helmets but includes a deep neck guard, lack of ear holes and a prominent brow ridge, all new innovations.

Plate 11: Soldier in *lorica squamata*. Scale armour was used extensively in the third century, individual scales are found on many military sites. This soldier wears a long hauberk of brass scale, he is also equipped with the *spatha* and a large oval shield. Like all shields in this period it is edged with rawhide, rather than the brass strips of the first and second centuries. The shield depicts Mars and the cockerel, unit symbol of *cohors* Quinta Gallorum, a fourth century auxiliary unit at the Roman fort South Shields, England. It is painted authentically, using hand-ground pigments dug from the ground and mixed with egg (used as a binding medium) by Paul Carrick. After aging a little, the paint becomes very hard and durable and virtually waterproof.

Plate 12: Ringmail Coif. The Battle of Ebenezer painting found within the synagogue of Dura Europus depicts soldiers wearing medieval-style coifs. Likely they were of scale, but here the soldier wears a ringmail coif, something certainly attested in the fourth century. Note the leather padding, essential if individual rings are to be prevented from being forced into the scalp from even a glancing blow. The spear is colourfully decorated, a custom known to have occurred in the fourth century and that may have begun in the third.

Plate 13: The penetrative power of a light *pilum* is tested against a rectangular *scutum*. The legionary *pilum* was designed with a long metal shank which allowed the javelin not just to hit a target and cause cutting and penetrative damage, but to provide an 'armour-piercing' warhead. If it did not hit flesh, but instead struck a shield, the shank was designed to punch through the board and then slide through to hopefully wound or kill the man behind it. This photograph is a graphic representation of that design in action. The tests were carried out by the Ancient History Department of Regensburg University in cooperation with the re-enactment group Legio III Italica Antoniniana. They went on to test the *scutum* against the penetration of arrows from a Roman recurve bow, they then set up a block of ballistic gelatine fronted by third century locked scale armour (over a *subarmalis* and woollen tunic). Arrows were shot and *pila* thrown at the test block revealing the terrible penetrative power of both. The *pilum* punched through the locked scale as if it was not there and a full 20 cm of the iron shank emerged from the back of the man-sized ballistic gelatine.

Plate 14: *Scutum* from Dura Europus. Found in tower 19 at Dura Europus, this rectangular Roman shield is so far the only surviving example from the imperial period. It is elaborately painted, with an eagle depicted at the top and a lion (perhaps a unit emblem) at the bottom. Gone are the lightning and thunderbolt motifs seen on shields of this type on Trajan's Column. The author's copy of this

shield can be seen in Colour Plate 8.
Plate 15: Tribune Terentius leads the Dura garrison in a religious ceremony. A wall painting from the Temple of Bel in Dura Europus. The scene shows tribune Julius Terentius, commander of the *cohors* XX Palmyrenorum, leading his men in worship. It provides a wealth of detail about the clothing and appearance of soldiers in this period. Note how Terentius and one other man (with fair hair, a European?) wear white cloaks, while the others wear shades of brown. Yet the commander retains the same style of tunic with a pair of pinkish-red stripes at the cuffs as the rest of his unit, perhaps his tunic is differentiated only by quality. Trousers are shades of grey and ring buckle belts are standard, with Terentius wearing a red-dyed belt, perhaps a further indicator of status. Despite the Syrian climate all men wear long-sleeved tunics and cloaks and most seem to be wearing sword baldrics although, again, that of the commander is coloured red. Terentius was killed during a Persian attack in 239.

Plate 16: Baldric Fitting. Open-work baldric decoration from Aldborough, northern England; almost identical designs have been found at Zugmantel in Germany. A copy of this fitting, in bronze, is worn by the soldier in colour plates 6 and 7. The Zugmantel example was found with a matching phalera featuring a Roman eagle. Both the phalera and the open-work baldric fitting include lettering which when read together asks for Jupiter's help in protecting the military unit of the wearer: OPTIME MAXIME CON(*serva*) NUMERUM OMNIUM MILITANTIUM.

Plate 17: Reconstructed Sword From Dura. This reconstructed sword and scabbard are based on finds from Dura Europus. The sword was made by Leo 'Tod' Todeschini for Dr Robert Mason of the Royal Ontario Museum. The blade was copied from the sword fragments from Dura, all of lenticular section. The original pommel was made of cut rock-crystal, Tod copied this in olive wood. Judging by other Roman sword finds, the guard would be of the same material and design as the pommel, and so that is how it has been reproduced. The guard plate of bronze and the grip of bone are copied from finds at Dura.

The scabbard has a wooden core, as one of the excavated sword finds showed traces of wood which had been spirally bound in cloth. Since there are no depictions of scabbards of this era that show spiral binding, it probably also had a leather covering. The scabbard slide and the chape are based on finds from Dura.

Plate 18: A decorated copper-alloy greave from a private collection in Germany. Lower leg protection was vital for frontline Roman troops. Although the press of men in that battle-line brought the fighters face-to-face, those in the second and third line were able to bend down and use spears or *pila* to stab at the legs of the Roman frontline. Other fighters in the frontline were able to target the vulnerable lower legs of Roman legionaries with spear or long sword since these vulnerable areas could not be protected by the shield. This example is unpublished and from the private collection of Mr Von Gravert . It was photographed here during a special exhibition in Speyer, Germany, during 2006.

Plate 19: Soldier wearing a brass manica on his sword-arm. It is likely that the *lorica segmentata* worn by the soldier in this photograph was inspired by segmented arm-guards (*manicae*) worn by gladiators in the Roman arena. The *manicae* appeared amongst the ranks too, coming to prominence on the Adamclissi sculptures from the Trajan Wars. The third century represents the pinnacle of personal protection and it is likely that many frontline troops wore *manicae* to protect their vulnerable right arms. A legionary on the Arch of Septimius Severus at Leptis Magna is depicted clad in *lorica segmentata* with a *manica* on his sword arm and the Alba Iulia sculpture is also wearing a *manica*. Archaeology has confirmed that the arm-guard was used through till the fourth century.

Plate 20: Chest Plates. A set of reconstructed chest plates in bronze, with much of the decoration tinned. Note the vertical locking pin which secures the two plates. Accepted opinion is that these act as a 'closure device' for the ringmail or scale, but practical experiments by the author and others have found that both of these armour types do not need any additional closure. The plates seem simply to be ornament, visible and ostentatious, and perhaps providing additional protection for the throat and sternum which is certainly vulnerable to sudden spear thrusts.

Plate 21: Spearman Fighting Overarm. Here a legionary fights overarm with his spear, the stance most often depicted in classical art. There are drawbacks to this technique, the most obvious (when compared with the underarm stance) is that the grip is midway down the shaft, greatly reducing the spear's reach. In addition the right arm and armpit is exposed to enemy attack. This fighting style probably represents the attacks of second rank troops who are able to fight overarm in order to reach over the shoulders of their comrades in the first rank.

Plate 22: Spearman Fighting Underarm. A legionary in ringmail wearing a brass Auxiliary Cavalry Type E helmet found at Kalkar-Hoenepel. The underarm fighting style is poorly attested in the records, yet it provides complete protection for the legionary and maximises the reach of his spear. A long reach reduces an enemy's ability to retaliate in combat and can keep cavalry at bay. Frontline

troops are most likely to have employed this fighting stance.
Plate 23: Spearman, View From the Front. This view of a legionary fighting underarm illustrates the protection afforded by the large oval shield, greaves and third century Auxiliary helmet. Only the right hand, the eyes, nose and mouth are exposed. The shield design is based on the Warrior God motif found on an example at Dura Europus; the green background on the original is here replaced with red.

Plate 24: Main colonnaded street of Palmyra, Syria.

Plate 25: Entrance to the hastily cut Roman counter-mine at Dura Europus.

Plate 26: The western ('desert') wall of Dura Europus which the Persian army attempted to undermine.

Plate 27: Sculpture at Naqsh-e Rostam, Iran, depicting the triumph of King Shapur I over the Roman Emperor Valerian.

Plate 28: Shapur I, king of Persia, on the face of a silver Sassanid coin.

Plate 29: The Aurelian Wall, commissioned by Emperor Aurelian after the Germanic invasions of Italy in 259 and 268. This 19 km wall was an admission that Rome could not depend on its armies for defence. Projecting towers studded the wall every 30 metres, and established buildings and monuments were built into the fabric of the fortifications. Eighteen gateways allowed access into the city through the wall.

Plate 30: A victim of one Germanic attack at Regensburg Harting in Germany. The ugly truth of the third century crisis. While we talk of sword types, emperors and Germanic incursions, people were dying – in large numbers. An ancient farming family from Raetia living around Regensburg-Harting were murdered by unknown assailants and recently found by archaeologists. Their skulls were smashed, the women had been scalped and the dead bodies were hacked into pieces and thrown down the local well. Archaeologists have identified evidence of scalping on this particular individual.

Bibliography

Ancient Sources

Ammianus Marcellinus
Aurelius Victor
Eutropius
Festus
Herodian
Josephus, *The Jewish War*
Livy, *The War with Hannibal*
Maurice, *Strategikon*
Malalas
Orosius
Scriptores Historiae Augustae
Severus Alexander
Tacitus, *Histories, Agricola*
Vegetius, *Epitoma Rei Militaris*
Zonaras
Zosimus, *New History*

Modern Sources

Birley, A. 1988. *The African Emperor, Septimius Severus.*
Bishop M. C. and J. C. N. Coulston. 2006. *Roman Military Equipment.*
Bohec, Y. le. 1994. *The Imperial Roman Army.*
Bowman, A. K. and Thomas, J. D. 1994. *The Vindolanda Writing Tablets* (Tabulae Vindolandenses II), pl. I, bottom.
Brauer, G. C. 1975. *The Age of the Soldier-Emperors.*
Campbell, J. B. 1984. *The Emperor and the Roman Army, 31 BC–AD 235*
Campbell, B. 1994. *The Roman Army, 31 BC–AD 337 A Sourcebook.*
Connolly, P. 1981. *Greece and Rome at War.*
Cornel, Tim and John Matthews. 1982. *Atlas of the Roman World.*

Cowan, E. 2002. Aspects of the Severan Field Army (PhD thesis, University of Glasgow).
Cowan, R. 2003. *Imperial Roman Legionary AD 161–284.*
Croom, A. T. 2000. *Roman Clothing and Fashion.*
Dandamaev, M.A., and Vladimir Lukonin. 1989. *The Culture and Social Institutions of Ancient Iran.*
Dodgeon, M. H. and Samuel N. C. Lieu (ed.) 1991. *The Roman Eastern Frontier and the Persian Wars, AD 226–363.*
Drinkwater, J. 2007. *The Alamanni and Rome.*
Elliott, P. 2007. *The Last Legionary.*
Elton, H. 1996. *Warfare in Roman Europe AD 350–425.*
Evans, R. 1986. *Soldiers of Rome.*
Farrokh, K. 2005. *Sassanian Elite Cavalry AD 224–642.*
Feugère, M. 2002. *Weapons of the Romans.*
Fink, R. O. 1971. *Roman Military Records on Papyrus.*
Goldsworthy, A. 2003. *The Complete Roman Army.*
Grant, M. 1968. *The Climax of Rome.*
Hekster, O. 2008. *Rome and its Empire, AD 193–284.*
Ibeji, M. 1991. *The Evolution of the Roman Army in the Third Century.*
James, Simon. 2004. *Excavations at Dura Europos, Final Report.*
James, Simon. 2011. *Rome and the Sword.*
Johnson, R. 2011. *The Afghan Way of War: How and Why They Fight.*
Le Blois, L. 1976. *The Policy of the Emperor Gallienus.*
Potter, D. 2004. *The Roman Empire at Bay: AD 180–395.*
Richmond, I. A. 1930. *The City Walls of Imperial Rome.*
Roaf, M. 1996. *Cultural Atlas of Mesopotamia.*
Robinson, H. R. 1975. *The Armour of Imperial Rome.*
Rostovtzeff, M. 1938. *Dura Europos and Its Art.*
Santosuosso, A. 2004. *Storming the Heavens.*
Southern, P. & K. R. Dixon. 1996. *The Late Roman Army.*
Southern, P. 2001. *The Roman Empire from Severus to Constantine.*
Speidel, M. 1994. *Riding for Caesar: The Roman Emperors' Horse Guard.*
Stark, F. 1966. *Rome on the Euphrates.*
Stephenson, I. P. 1999. *Roman Infantry Equipment: The Later Empire.*
Stephenson, I. P. 2006. *Romano-Byzantine Infantry Equipment.*
Stoneman, R. 1992. *Palmyra and its Empire.*
Sumner, G. 1997. *Roman Army: Wars of the Empire.*
Sumner, G. 2009. *Roman Military Dress.*
Watson, A. 1999. *Aurelian and the Third Century.*
Webster, G. 1981. The Roman Imperial Army.
Wiesehöfer, J. 1996. *Ancient Persia.*
Wilcox, P. 1986. *Rome's Enemies 3: Parthians and Sassanid Persians.*
Woolf, G. 1998. *Becoming Roman: The Origins of Provincial Civilization in Gaul.*

Endnotes

Chapter 1: The Rise of Septimius Severus

1. During his stay, the emperor is said to have resided in a *domus palatina* or palace, but no trace of such a building has been found in York. More likely then, the commander's house (*praetorium*) served as the imperial residence.
2. Herodian 3.15
3. The three legions of Syria were III Gallica at Raphanaea, IV Scythica at Zeugma and XVI Flavia Firma at Samosata.
4. The three legions garrisoned in Upper Pannonia were I Adiutrix at Brigetio, X Gemina at Vindobona and XIIII Gemina at Carnuntum.
5. Dio Cassius 75.1 reports that 'the spectacle proved the most brilliant of any that I have witnessed; for the whole city had been decked with garlands of flowers and laurel and adorned with richly coloured stuffs, and it was ablaze with torches and burning incense; the citizens, wearing white robes and with radiant countenances, uttered many shouts of good omen.' This seems too good to be true, for everyone's thoughts must have been on the fate of the Roman city of Cremona, sacked and destroyed by victorious legions during the civil war of AD 69.
6. The Praetorian Guard was led by an imperial appointee, the praetorian prefect, and made up of ten cohorts, each led by one tribune and six centurions. Cohorts may have been 500 or 1,000 man strong, varying from reign to reign. Many emperors made changes to the Guard.
7. The Latin word *miles* (plural *milite*') was the term for a trained Roman soldier, while a new recruit was referred to as a *tiro*. It is this word for the Roman soldiery, the *milites,* from which we derive the word 'military'.

Chapter 2: New Strategies

1. Vegetius I.5; this practice was also used in the grenadier companies of eighteenth and nineteenth century armies which selected tall and strong men in order that the unit might act as a striking force.

2. According to Robert Johnson, using data from the United Nations Assistance Mission in Afghanistan (UNAMA 2010), 'ANA recruits were young, three in ten were drug addicts, nine out of ten were illiterate and 25 per cent per year were prone to desertion. Amongst the embedded training teams (the Operational Mentoring and Liaison Teams or Collective Training Teams) few Western military advisors believed that Afghan units were capable of fighting the insurgents without Western forces being present.' Johnson, R. 2011. The Afghan Way of War: How and Why They Fight.
3. Batavian auxiliaries, recruited from the warlike Batavi tribe at the mouth of the Rhine, made up eight infantry cohorts within the Roman army. In AD 69 relations between the Batavi auxiliaries and the Roman government collapsed. Led by a Batavi prince-turned cohort commander with the adopted name of Gaius Julius Civilis, the auxiliaries rebelled and defeated two legions, V Alaudae and XV Primigenia in battle. (Tacitus. *Histories*. 4.12)
4. Tombstone CIL VI 2553: D(is) M(anibus). / P(ublio) Aelio Maximino, mil(iti) / coh(ortis) V pr(aetoriae) p(iae) v(indicis), ex 7 (centuria) Mo/ ni, qui vix(it) ann(os) XXXI, / mensib(us) VIII, militavit / ann(os) XII. Omnibus expeditionibus functo / Aurelius Sextianus com / manipulus et heres eius / contubernali rarissimo / posuit.
5. Herodian 3.9.2
6. Ibeji, M. The Evolution of the Roman Army in the Third Century. 1991. also Campbell, D. *Coinage and Cavalry: The sources for Gallienus and his equites*, Ancient Warfare, Dec/Jan 2009, pp. 8-11.
7. Inscription CIL VI 41271: memorial to the procurator Lucius Gallus Iulianus, who repelled the Costoboci invasion of the Balkans in AD 170, tempore belli Germanici et Sarmatici ('at the time of the German and Sarmatian War').
8. Ammianus Marcellenus 17.12
9. Ammianus Marcellinus 17.12
10. Elton, H. 1996. Warfare in Roman Europe 350–425. p. 67

Chapter 3: The Crisis Begins

1. Herodian 5.8
2. Ammianus Marcellenus 23.5
3. Zosimus I. 28-29; Orosius 7.22; Eutropius 9.7; Aurelius Victor 32

Chapter 4: Appearance of the Soldiers

1. Sumner, G. 2009. Roman Military Dress. pp. 119-144
2. Numerous pieces of sculpture seem to flirt with this convention, the most telling of which are the legionaries depicted on the Adamklissi monument

which was sculpted by the soldiers themselves. In one scene several soldiers carrying curved shields are shown marching and each wears his *gladius* on his left side.

3. Representations of *bracae* occur both on the Tropaeum Traiani at Adamklissi, and Trajan's Column in Rome.
4. Simon James. 2004. Excavations at Dura Europos, Final Report, 2004. p. 59.
5. *Historia Augusta*, Severus Alexander, 40.11. Alexander is also said to have given away clothing to the soldiers. 'He would also give away equipment for the troops, such as leggings, trousers, and boots.' ('*donavit et ocreas et bracas et calciamenta inter vestimenta militaria.*') *Historia Augusta*, Severus Alexander, 40.5
6. C.van Driel-Murray and M.Gechter. 1994. 'The Leatherwork' in *Funde aus der Fabrica der Legio I Minervia am Bonner Berg*, in Beiträge zur Archäeologie des Römischen Rheinlandes 4, 'The generally accepted archaeological division into military boots (*caligae*), closed shoes (*calcei*), sandals (*soleae*), sewn slippers (*socci*) and one piece shoes (*carbatinae*), is retained for convenience...It is unlikely that the varied foorwear ... would all have been termed as such by the Romans themselves, but the terms are commonly accepted.'
7. Bowman, A. K. and Thomas, J. D. 1994. The Vindolanda Writing Tablets (Tabulae Vindolandenses II), pl. I, bottom
8. Rome, Vatican Museums, after Speidel, M. 1994. *Riding for Caesar: The Roman Emperors' Horse Guard.*
9. Simon James, *Op.cit.* p. 251.
10. *Historia Augusta*, Daturninus, 23.5
11. Portrait of a soldier dressed in a white tunic with a red cloak, painted on linen, from Deir el-Medineh, Egypt. Some cloaks, like the one worn by Aurelius Lucianus at Rome, sported a fringed hem while a small number had a tassel on each lower edge.
12. Wild, J.P. 1968. *'Clothing in the north-west provinces of the roman empire'*, in Bonner Jahrbücher 168, pp. 166-240.
13. Sumner, G. *Op.cit.*

Chapter 5: Sword and Shield

1. Tacitus, Agricola 36
2. Connolly. P. 1981. Greece and Rome at War, p. 233.
3. Of course the use of sword or spear was dictated by the situation, or the orders of the day. Agricola at Mons Graupius, for example 'exhorted the four Batavian and two Tungrian cohorts to fight hand to hand at sword's point. They had trained for this during their long military service... So the

Batavians rained blows indiscriminately, struck with their shield bosses and stabbed in the face.' Tacitus, Agricola 36.

4. Bishop, M. and John Coulston. 2006. *Roman Military Equipment*, pp. 233-240.
5. James, S. 2004. *Op.cit.* pp. 251-254.
6. Although undated, the Aquincum soldier wears a ring-pommel sword on a baldric, but also wears the distinctive hanging apron of leather straps worn by Roman troops no later than the mid-second century.
7. Bishop, M. and John Coulston. 2006. Roman Military Equipment, p. 163.
8. James, S. 2011. Rome and the Sword, p. 185.
9. Coulston, J. 1983. *Arms and Armour in Sculpture* in M. C. Bishop (ed.), Roman Military Equipment: Proceedings of a seminar held in the department of Ancient History and Classical Archaeology at the University of Sheffield.
10. James, S. 2004. *Op.cit.* p.184-186; note that the shield numbering system used in the Final Report is referenced here.
11. Simon James. 2011. *Op.cit.* p. 187
12. For the use and effects of the *spatha,* see Vegetius 1.12, Ammianus 15.5, 16.12, 25.3 and 31.13.
13. Stephenson, I. 1999. Roman Infantry Equipment, p. 71.

Chapter 6: Battlefield Protection

1. Robinson, H.R. 1975. The Armour of Imperial Rome.
2. RIB 1914; dated: c. AD 219.
3. Kestroi 1.1.50-52
4. Anonymous, De Rebus Bellicis, 15.1-2; for details of the felt backing at Dura see James, S. 2004. *Op.cit.* p. 116, item 379; the body and the armour was probably Persian.
5. These experiences come from a climb of England's highest mountain, Scafell Pike (978 metres), in Cumbria, while wearing third century scale armour and carrying shields, swords and spears. This was successfully attempted in January 2005 by Jamie McLean, 'Doc' and Ingrid Shackleton, Paul Elliott and friends. The route began at Hardknott Roman fort and followed the River Esk as far as the Great Moss boggy plateau. From there the walkers ascended up to Mickledore, the low ridge between Sca Fell and Scafell Pike, from where the summit was then reached.
6. ILS 8878
7. Fernández, J.A. 2007. *Las Armaduras Segmentadas (Loricae Segmentatae) en los yacimientos romanos de la provincia de León*, in Archivo Español de Arqueología, pp. 153-182
8. Ammianus Marcellenus 31.13

Chapter 7: Other Weapons

1. Herodian 4.10.
2. Stephenson, I. 2006. Romano-Byzantine Infantry Equipment; Wheeler, E.L. 2004. *The Legion as Phalanx in the Late Empire* 2, in Revue des Études Militaires Anciennes 1, pp. 147-75; Wheeler says that 'many scholars now accept the phalangical formation of (spear-wielding) Roman/Byzantine heavy infantry for pitched battles in the fourth century through the early seventh centuries'
3. Herodian 4.15
4. Tombstone AE 1993, 1575, reads: D(is) M(anibus) / [A]ur(eli) M(u)ciani quondam dis/centi(s) lanc{h}iari(orum) leg(ionis) II Part(hicae) / |(centuria) VIIII pil(i) pr(ioris) qui milit[avit] ann(os) X / vixit ann(os) XXX c[ontu]ber(nali?) / optimo Septim[ius ---] dup/l(icarius) leg(ionis) s(upra) s(criptae) |(centuria) VIII p[--- b(ene)] m(erenti) f(ecit).
5. Cassius Dio 69.15; also Acies contra Alanos.
6. Wheeler, E.L. 2004. *The Legion as Phalanx in the Late Empire 1* in de IIIe congrès de Lyon sur l'armée romaine, ed. Le Bohec, Y. also see Wolff, C. 1998. Becoming Roman: The Origins of Provincial Civilization in Gaul. pp. 309-58.
7. Bishop, M. and John Coulston, 2006. Op.cit. p. 150
8. Malalas 12

Chapter 8: The Soldier's Experience

1. Forni, G. 1953. Il relutamento delle legioni da Augusto a Diocleziano.
2. Vegetius 1.3.
3. M. Bishop & John Coulston. 2006. *Op.cit.* pp. 254-259.
4. Josephus, *The Jewish War* 6.61; the tombstone of Titus Aurelius Flavinus is listed as ILS 7178 and AE 1961, 208.
5. Goldsworthy, A. 2003. The Complete Roman Army, pp. 102-103.
6. Josephus, *The Jewish War, 3.87*

Chapter 9: The Persian Onslaught

1. Eunapius vitae Sophistarum, 6.5 and Zosimus 3.32.
2. Inscription of Shapur at the Kaaba of Zoroastre; 'Res Gesate Divi Saporis', ed. and trans. A. Maricq. Syria 35, 1958, p. 245-60.
3. Zonaras 12, 23, p. 593 and p. 595.
4. Aurelius Victor, 'liberde Caesaribus' 32, 5; Lactantius, 'de mortibus persecutorum' 5.

5. Rostovtzeff, M. 1938. Dura Europos and Its Art; see also Baird, J.A. 2011, *Photographing Dura-Europos, 1928-1937. An Archaeology of the Archive* in American Journal of Archaeology 115.3, p. 427-46.
6. For a discussion of troop numbers and details of the Dura garrison see Simon James. 2004. *Op.cit. pp. 14-25.*

Chapter 10: Restitutor Orbis

1. *Historia Augusta, The Life of Claudius*
2. Richmond, I. A. 1930. The City Walls of Imperial Rome, p. 67.
3. Festus, *Breviarium*, 9.15
4. Eutropius, *Breviarium,* 9.13
5. Shapur I probably died in 272, he was succeeded by his youngest son Hormid I who had served as governor of Khorasan. Bahram I, who was Shapur's eldest son, then ruled Persia until his death in 276. Bahram's own son, Bahram II, then became king until his death in 293.

Chapter 11: Epilogue: Into the Fourth Century

1. Bishop, M. and John Coulston. 2006. *Op.cit. pp.* 200-227.
2. An excellent sculptural rendering of an Intercisa style helmet was found on a gravestone from Gamzigrad, in Serbia; two other helmets feature on wall-paintings from Roman catacombs, one from the Via Latina Catacomb, the other from the Via Maria Catacomb.

Index